Alfred Garnett Mortimer

The Laws of Happiness

Or the Beatitudes as Teaching our Duty to God, Self and our Neighbour

Alfred Garnett Mortimer

The Laws of Happiness
Or the Beatitudes as Teaching our Duty to God, Self and our Neighbour

ISBN/EAN: 9783337232030

Printed in Europe, USA, Canada, Australia, Japan

Cover: Foto ©Thomas Meinert / pixelio.de

More available books at **www.hansebooks.com**

THE LAWS OF HAPPINESS;

OR,

THE BEATITUDES

AS TEACHING OUR DUTY TO GOD,
SELF AND OUR NEIGHBOUR.

BY THE

REV. ALFRED G. MORTIMER, B. D.,

Rector of S. Mary's, Castleton, N. Y.

NEW YORK:
E. & J. B. YOUNG & CO.,
Cooper Union.
1888.

COPYRIGHT

1888,

BY ALFRED G. MORTIMER.

TO THE ASSOCIATES OF THE

SISTERHOOD OF S. MARY,

IN MEMORY OF

THE RETREATS AT PEEKSKILL AND KENOSHA,

THESE ADDRESSES ARE AFFECTIONATELY

DEDICATED.

PREFACE.

In sending forth these addresses on the Beatitudes I desire to add a few words of explanation and apology.

In 1883 the line of thought here worked out was indicated in some Meditations published in Volume II. of my "Helps to Meditation." These thoughts were afterwards used in Retreats given to the Associates of the Sisterhood of S. Mary at Peekskill and at Kenosha, and in a Retreat at Toronto. Having been requested by many to publish them I gave them as a series of addresses in my own Parish Church last Fall, and arranged to have a stenographer report them. I publish them now without any attempt to rewrite them, having merely corrected the stenographer's notes. They thus exhibit faults of style which belong to extempore preaching, but in spite of this I have felt that they would be more acceptable in this form to those who had heard them delivered, than they would be if I rewrote them. My apology for publishing them must be the requests of many friends, the fact that I have been unable to find any little book on the Beatitudes which gives them more than the most superficial treatment, and that I believe that their more careful study would be helpful to all.

ALFRED G. MORTIMER.

S. MARY'S RECTORY,
WEST NEW BRIGHTON, S. I., NEW YORK.
Epiphany, 1888.

CONTENTS.

	PAGE
Introduction	1
First Beatitude	7
Second Beatitude	18
Third Beatitude	32
Fourth Beatitude	44
Fifth Beatitude	58
Sixth Beatitude	71
Seventh Beatitude	84
Eighth Beatitude	99

INTRODUCTORY ADDRESS.

EVERY system of religion, every school of philosophy, has started out to investigate and to teach the way of happiness, has attempted to answer the question: What is the happy life, the life worth living? When our Lord opened His mouth and taught the multitude, saying, "Blessed," He used a word which at once awoke in the minds of His hearers the familiar though perplexing controversy—how is man to attain to happiness? That he was made for happiness every faculty of his being insisted, but among all those many roads labelled by different schools, "To Happiness," which was the right road. That was the question which each new school of thought set itself to answer. And so when our Lord on the very threshold of His work, and on an occasion of special publicity, began His discourse with that familiar word μακαρίος, all listened without surprise but with peculiar attention as He pointed out the way and promulgated the laws which in this new school of religion He promised should lead men to happiness.

"*By their fruits ye shall know them.*" Years have passed sufficient for these various schools to bring forth their fruit, to fulfil their promise or to stand convicted of failure, and as we scan the fields of history what do we see? Glorious representatives of each school upon whose brows the world with united acclaim has placed the crown of genius. Men who by the brilliance of their intellect, by their indomitable perseverance in the pursuit of knowledge, by their splendid patriotism, have been benefactors both of their country and of their race. Men who have stored up vast treasures of knowledge which they have left as a rich legacy to the world. But happiness! the harmonizing of the discord in the human soul, the satisfying the cravings of the human heart, the answer to the perplexities of the human mind—that which their school promises as its end, happiness! We read in every such life disappointment, the fatal word, " Failure !" How is it that outside of Christianity a gloom almost like that of Calvary shrouds the spirits of the greatest of the world's heroes; that genius apart from Christ wears always the amaranthine wreath of sadness. Brilliant discoveries in the fields of science, magnificent inductions in the realms of thought appreciable by the few, but that which the heart of every man cries for—happiness! met either by the confession that it is as yet unattained or by the assertion that it is unattainable.

One exception alone to this rule, the experience of the Saints, who, not drawn from any one class of men but fairly representing human nature, join in the one shout, $E\breve{v}\rho\eta\varkappa\alpha$! Intellects as powerful as St. Augustine's, or as simple as St. Francis of Assisi's. Natures as cultured as St. Elizabeth's of Hungary, or as inured to hardness as St. Anthony of the desert. Men of every temperament, rank, or station, proclaim that independent of all the circumstances of their lives, in the practice of the laws of sanctity, in the fulfilment of the commandments of Christ, they have found all He promised,—happiness here, and they have sunk to their rest in the firm assurance of happiness in eternity. All, independent of the accidents of mere external life, all who have honestly lived by the laws of Beatitude promulgated in the Sermon on the Mount, have witnessed that the troubles of life have been robbed of their sting, that they have found a happiness, which has satisfied every craving of their souls, and which has endured.

Then to turn from the testimony of individual experience to the evidence of the world at large. Does it not owe a great part of its present happiness, or at least the amelioration of much of its misery to that Christianity which, although it has been but a partial carrying out of the Great Founder's laws, has still brought abundant blessings on the human race?

These things being so, let us begin for ourselves the study of our Lord's epitome of the laws of happiness, not paring down their demands to our weakness, not emptying them of their meaning so as to bring them within the reach of our self-indulgent lives, but rising up to their claims upon us in full confidence that grace will be given to all who earnestly seek it

Introduction. 5

to pass through the strait gate and to tread the narrow way which leads to happiness.

"*He went up into a mountain: and when He was set, His disciples came unto Him: and He opened His mouth and taught them, saying,* "*Blessed.*"

The scene carries our thoughts back to the occasion of the giving of the law of the Old Dispensation, when Moses went up into the Mount and received from GOD the ten commandments. But while we are struck by the external resemblance of the circumstances we must not fail also to notice the contrast, the one given amid the thunders and lightnings which typified the terrors of the Law. The other amid the calmness and simplicity which fitted the Gospel of Peace. The one, a law of negative commandment, "*Thou shalt not;*" the other of positive promise, "*Blessed are they.*"

To my mind, one of the greatest mistakes people generally make in studying the Beatitudes, is that they consider them separately, as though they were a series of isolated promises, instead of a complete revelation, as if they were strung together in arbitrary order instead of succeeding one another in strict and necessary sequence.

Let us study them now as a miniature, but systematic treatise on the spiritual life, indeed as giving us, arranged in the most symmetrical order, the laws of a happy life.

We have only three possible relationships in life,—towards GOD, ourself and our neighbour. The first three Beatitudes give us the passive side of our duty to each of these respectively and (excluding the eighth as not strictly one of the chain) they correspond inversely to the last three which give the active side of the same duties. The fourth or central Beatitude forms as it were the balance in the scale of sanctity, the apex of the pyramid of duty, the sides of which correspond as negative and positive aspects of the three relationships of life; and is at the same time the test and result of the first three, the spring and cause of the last three— while the eighth we may regard—not so much as a law of spiritual life—as a prophecy of the result both here and hereafter of a faithful fulfilment of all the seven.

FIRST BEATITUDE.

"*Blessed are the poor in spirit: for their's is the kingdom of heaven.*"

Our Lord begins with a paradox, Blessed are the πτωχοί, the beggars in spirit—for such is the meaning of πτωχεία—not merely poverty, having little—but having nothing and depending on the gifts of another for the very necessities of life.

Let us begin by considering what is included in this poverty in spirit which our Lord tells us is the first law of true happiness.

It cannot necessarily mean external poverty—for that is consistent and indeed often found linked with pride or covetousness—while this is the beatitude of humility. The words, "in spirit," which are added to qualify the term poor, show the sphere in which that poverty is to exist, that it is interior poverty.

It is self-knowledge, for coming into GOD's

Presence we see ourselves as we are—it is the recognition of the truth as to what we are, and what we have. That we have nothing of our own, that we are but stewards, and hence at the outset it forces upon us a sense of our responsibility.

We are stewards and some part at least of the parable of the Unjust Steward we may apply to ourselves, all of it we may regard as a most solemn warning, for to each of us will one day be said, "*Give an account of thy stewardship.*" If we are to give an account we must keep an account here, therefore we are taught the practical importance of self-examination in order that our account may be always ready for the scrutiny of our Lord.

This realization of the truth as to what we have—that we have nothing of our own but that all is GOD's—must make us willing to give up what GOD sees fit to withdraw from us, must teach us to sit loosely to all the creatures around us, must call us to the practice of detachment. Not anticipating the call of GOD and putting away from us the good things GOD has given us to enjoy, but while using all He has given with gratitude, using them also in a spirit of dependence, watching lest we begin to look upon as our own what is only loaned to us, training our soul in the attitude of dependence on GOD for all things, in the attitude of detachment to all creatures, using, but not over using and so abusing them, remembering that as stewards, "*it is required that a man be found faithful.*"

A step lower on the ladder of poverty is reached when we have come to realize that the creatures around us are nothing apart from GOD; for they will all pass away, and their very beauty they derive from their capacity to reflect something of GOD. Take for example an atom of dust and a beautiful flower. The force by which that atom of dust is enabled to manifest itself is as much a part of GOD's power as the force which holds the planets in their wondrous course; for when we speak of GOD as Almighty we do not so much mean that He can do all things, as that nothing can be done without Him, and that all power is GOD's power. Or take the beauty of colour in the rich damask of the rose, or the delicate tints of the Passion flower, what is it but the result of a capacity for absorbing certain colour rays. The colour is in the ray of light, the flower owes its beauty of colour to its inability freely to absorb that colour.

So let us regard the world around us, recognizing more and more that the only possible possession of the soul is GOD, the only true riches, those which will endure beyond the grave.

The first beatitude puts the soul in its true attitude to GOD, sweeping away all that might come between the soul and GOD, and more—purifying the very atmosphere through which we regard GOD. All theology must begin with right views of GOD. Every spiritual life must be built up on a recognition of the soul's true relation to GOD. Blessed are the poor in spirit! Happy are the beggars! Happy in the realisation of their complete dependence on GOD, in the thought that all that they have is GOD's—more, that they themselves are His.

Yes, this poverty is the dethronement of sin and self, the emptying of the soul that it may be filled with GOD. "*Open wide thy mouth and I will fill it.*" How often there is no room for GOD's blessings because we do not open *wide* our mouths.

We must remember too that one day we must be filled with GOD or with Satan. Man is so created that he cannot stand alone. His soul is the battle ground on which meet not merely the powers of good and evil, but the Holy One and the Evil One.

Man is a person, and when we utter the word its derivation from "*persona*" carries us back to the masks which the actors in the Classic drama wore, and behind which they acted the character they assumed; so is man a mask in which the ultimate actor is GOD or the Devil. Perhaps our Lord would teach us this in that striking scene on the coasts of Gadara, in which we see so vividly portrayed the only two possible goals of man.

In the early morning light He approaches the city of Gadara. There meets Him a poor devil-possessed man, whose abode was in the tombs and whose sufferings are described with peculiar and graphical clearness by St. Luke. The man falls at our Lord's feet. What a picture! What a parable! What a revelation! For there we see the utmost possibilities of humanity in either direction. At the one extreme the poor demoniac sunk so low that his soul is possessed by the devil, at the other extreme standing over him, speaking words of pity and love, the Incarnate Son of GOD, man possessed by GOD. On the one hand we see man raised to his highest possibilities, on the other sunk to his lowest degradation, and we are all of us now standing somewhere between these two extremes. To which are we tending? Are we by the continual yielding of our will to temptation allowing Satan to get such possession of us that our history will be but a record of downward descent until we are entirely devil-possessed, until we lose the wish to do one right deed, or having the wish have lost the power of ever gratifying it by one good act. Or on the other hand are we, though perhaps through many falls, still struggling upwards, "*forgetting those things which are behind, and reaching forth unto those things which are before.*" Are we pressing "*toward the mark for the prize of the high calling of God in Christ Jesus*" until our will is so conformed to GOD's will, our nature so assimilated to Christ's nature through the working of His Holy Spirit, that we at length find our joy in being possessed by

GOD, and for eternity. And this, the highest hope of the human heart, the topmost pinnacle of human sanctity, this has as its foundation the clear grasp of the true relation in which we stand to GOD. The discovery of our own nothingness apart from Him, of our wondrous possibilities when united to Him, of the splendid destiny of man as purposed by the predestinating love of GOD. It is the discovery of a new object in life, a turning away from the creatures on account of their nothingness, and a directing of the soul to GOD.

This beatitude then gives us the true attitude of the soul to GOD. We must learn it first, as the first table of the law which contains man's duty to GOD comes necessarily before the second table which teaches his duty to his neighbour. And the thorough recognition of our entire dependence on GOD is not only necessary as the only possible starting point in the way of holiness but it is, as the beatitude says, Happiness. Happy are the beggars in spirit, for it is to be at once free from all the cares of life, it is to cast all our cares on Him who careth for us.

How deeply touching is that saying of St.

Peter, "*Casting all your care on Him for He careth for you,*" and how beautifully the Holy Spirit through St. Peter teaches us how we may cast our cares on GOD, it is but another way of putting this beatitude. Be ye clothed with humility; put on the ἐγκόμβωμα of humility, the livery which proclaims that you belong to GOD, and what is that livery but humility. Just as the slave wore the εγκόρβωρα which marked him out as a slave, and perhaps by some peculiarity showed to what great house he belonged, and therefore protected him; so does humility, poverty of spirit mark us out as the δοῦλοι of GOD, the bond servants of Christ, and therefore under His special protection. Well may we cast our cares on Him. It was the solitary privilege of the slave amid many miseries to be able to look to his master for all his needs, how much more is it the glorious privilege of the children of GOD to be able to cast all their cares on Him. Only they must put on His ἐγκόμβωμα which is humility, they must be poor in spirit.

We read of our Lord that He began *to do* and to teach. In all His teaching, we may look to the *example* of the Teacher. As St. Paul says, "Ye know the grace of our Lord Jesus Christ, that though He was rich, yet for your sakes He became poor (ἐπτώχευσεν.)

He emptied Himself of worldly estate, of royal glory, even of the human sympathy He craved, He was poor in spirit. His was the example of the Blessed Life. Am I following this example? What am I living for? Is covetousness the ruling passion of my life, the love of seeming to possess those creatures which really belong to GOD, and not one of which I can carry with me into the life beyond the grave; or is it ambition, the ruling passion of noble souls, as the world calls it? Read the history of gratified ambition in the lives of the world's heroes, in the biographies of those who climbed successfully, though painfully, to the very summit of fame's ladder—to find what? Disappointment—that the prize, which in the distance seemed like pure gold, was but the gilt of earth, that the world they loved so much had turned to dust and ashes at their touch. Is it pleasure, the butterfly life of the frivolous and superficial?

How soon pleasure's glow passes away!

How soon its brighest flowers fade and wither and decay. Or on the other hand am I poor in spirit, realising that I am but GOD's steward, willing to give up all if GOD so wills, finding my joy in resting upon the broad ocean of His Providence? This is indeed the Blessed Life, the life without care, without disappointment. And what is the special reward? "*Blessed are the poor in spirit: for their's is the kingdom of heaven.*" The kingdom of heaven as contrasted with the kingdom of this world which the πτωχοί have surrendered;- for the two can no more co-exist in the same heart than light and darkness in the same place. But the capacity for assimilating Christ's Kingdom depends upon this emptiness of soul. It was not until the famine was sore in the land of Canaan that Joseph's brethren were driven to seek the bread which he alone could give, and in the attainment of which they found peace and restoration. It was not until the prodigal son had tried to satisfy the pangs of hunger with the husks which the swine did eat—had tried and failed—that he said, "*I will arise and go to my father.*" The five thousand whom our Lord fed so miraculously in the wilderness had this special characteristic, that they were fasting from earthly food, that they had left their homes to seek Him. Yes, that kingdom of heaven, which, our Lord says, cometh not with observation but is within you, depends on there being room in your soul for the things of heaven, requires you to fast from the mere things of earth.

Let us pray that GOD may give us grace to see ourselves, as we really are, as beggars in His sight—not that we may murmur at our nothingness but that we may rejoice in the claims which that very nothingness gives us on GOD.

Lord! amid all life's storms, in its bitterest struggles, Thou hast revealed the secret of happiness—to be beggars in spirit that we may cast all our cares on Thee; for Thou carest for us.

THE SECOND BEATITUDE.

"*Blessed are they that mourn : for they shall be comforted.*"

The first three beatitudes give us the *passive* side of our duty to GOD, ourself and our neighbour. And as the first teaches us the true attitude of our soul to GOD, the recognition of our own nothingness and of our absolute dependence on Him for everything; so in the second beatitude do we learn the right attitude of the soul towards itself—a spirit of penitence.

"*Blessed are they that mourn ;*" for this is the foundation of all personal sanctity, the passive virtue corresponding to, and the spring of, that active purity of heart which enables the soul to see GOD.

How strange does this law of happiness sound to the world's ears. Happy are they that mourn ! Are not happiness and mourning mutually contradictory?

The world says, get all the pleasure you can out of life, put off its sorrows, avoid them as long as you can. Our Lord on the other hand, as one of the fundamental laws of His Kingdom, says, look the truth in the face, this world is a vale of tears; but as the storms of winter and the showers of spring prepare the way for the glorious verdure and the brilliant flowers of summer, so beneath the sorrows of life lie hid the elements of all future joy.

"*Blessed are they that mourn.*" Consider what the soul sees around it in this world, one phenomenon everywhere, a mystery of tears. Yes, sorrow is the king here below, and sooner or later every heart is touched by his sceptre. Oh, how soon the face which is wreathed in smiles is bathed in tears! How soon upon the youthful memory is ploughed the recollections of sorrow. One phenomenon everywhere, a mystery of tears, one mark deep stamped upon the soul of each child of man, the mark of sorrow. And then the soul sees one universal fact to account for all this, the fact of sin. Not only the withered leaves which the autumn winds bring rustling around our feet, not only the crumbling ruins of ancient buildings, not only the pain-stricken frames of the sufferers in our hospitals, but even in heaven itself the empty thrones from which the angels fell all bear witness to that fact, which is the universal cause of all this phenomenon of sorrow, the fact of SIN. And yet again we see one common result, GOD dishonoured, man ruined.

"*Blessed are they that mourn,*" says our Lord. Blessed are they who recognise this fact and do not try, as the multitude, to ignore it, do not try to hide it beneath the glittering excitements of the world's pleasures, do not endeavour to drown it beneath the wild surges of the world's passions, but bend their backs to the burden of the world's cross, open their hearts in sympathy to the world's sorrows, and following the example of the Man of Sorrows, mourn for the world.

What a wonderful thing sympathy is. Sympathy! word of magic power, which unlocks the hardened heart, and compels the tears to flow. Sympathy which shares the burden of sorrow and gives strength to bear it. Sympathy which makes us indeed the ministers of Christ, which makes us willing to carry on the work of Christ even in its humblest form. If we visit the poor and sorrowful and sick, the power which makes us good visitors is sympathy—to listen again and again to the same old story of sorrow, disappointment and pain, to listen and not find it wearisome just because we love souls so deeply, just because our sympathy is so great, that is the power which enables us to mourn for the sins of the world, which helps us to bear one another's burdens; that is the power our Lord speaks of when He says, " Happy are they that mourn."

But let us consider for what we have to mourn:

First for our own sins, for our own failures—that having such desire to do right, having born within us such a love of GOD, having vouchsafed to us such a clear recognition of our duty, and having bestowed upon us such boundless treasures of grace to enable us to do that duty, yet we still fail so often and so sadly. Can we do anything but mourn, when we think of ourselves? When we look back, perhaps on the days of our youth, and recall all the splendid schemes we then had for the glory of GOD, and the good of mankind, and see now how few of them begun, how very few, even of those that were begun, have ever been finished.

And again if we are to enter into the spirit of Christ, if we are to fulfil the law of Christ, we must bear one another's burdens, we must mourn for our brother's sorrows, and deeply mourn for his inability so often to make them what GOD means them to be, remedial. The true way to look upon the greater part of the sufferings of life, is that they are meant to be remedial, to blunt and check what is wrong in us. If they sometimes damp or crush our buoyant spirits, it is that we may have a truer view of life, even if it be a sadder one, that we may not be misled by the mere butterfly view of life which so many take, but opening our eyes to the world's unreality and disappointment, we may enter on the duties of life realising the truth. Not crushed by it, but mellowed, deepened, sanctified by sorrow and suffering. Having that happiness which comes from a conviction that sorrow in this world can only touch the outer life, and that if we have in the secret chamber of our souls Jesus, the Prince of Peace, though our eyes may weep at the sin and suffering we see, yet we may always find peace and joy in Him, and repose in the certainty that all sorrow shall be turned into joy.

Again we must mourn for this dying world in which we are, mourn for its inability to recognise the truth, mourn to see it so occupied in arraying itself in its grave-clothes that it allows to escape out of its hands, that life, that eternal life, which is within its grasp.

What a strange scene this world is. So like some drama, which, while deeply touching, we know to be utterly unreal. We see the world moving on, individuals coming upon the stage and playing their part, a few here and there in earnest, but the majority living the butterfly life of mere excitement, of striving for worldly success, of straining to reach some object of worldly ambition, to gain some worldly prize, which when it seems within reach, either eludes their grasp or crumbles to dust as they seize it.

So we begin to see what our Lord means

when He says, "Happy are they that mourn." He does not mean to say we are to go through life in a spirit of bitterness. There is no bitterness in the gentle mourning of which He speaks. He says go through life not refusing to see its sorrow, but doing what you can to alleviate those sorrows, to mourn with those that mourn, and by your sympathy to comfort them.

But again we may ask, how are we to mourn? for it certainly is not every kind of mourning that our Lord pronounces blessed. There are some tears, so passionate, so bitter, that we can see no possibility of happiness in them. If we are to mourn aright, it must be in the spirit of penitence. There were two thieves crucified with our Lord, the one reviled Him in the bitterness of his agony, the other suffering no whit less pain, said, "*We receive the due reward of our deeds*," and mourned in the spirit of penitence. So it is not mourning in a spirit of bitter complaint at the unsatisfactoriness and unreality of all around us, but it is that mourning which recognises the claims which the world's sorrows have on every Christian heart. "*I did mourn as a dove*," says the prophet, Isaiah.

Yes, it is this mourning in the spirit of The Dove, the Holy Ghost, Whose Office it is to convince the world of sin, Who is the Spirit of Penitence. And if we mourn in reliance on the Holy Ghost, the spirit of penitence will help us to bear our sorrows aright, and will make each one a blessing to us. And from this we naturally pass to the reward promised. "*Blessed are they that mourn: for they shall be comforted,*" for it is the Office of the Dove, the Holy Ghost, to be the Comforter, but it is only those who mourn as doves, that is, in the spirit of penitence who can expect to experience in their own souls, that sweet work of Comfort. The Holy Ghost then will be our Comforter; for the spirit of penitence will lead us to the spirit of peace; penitence, which insures forgiveness of sin, absolving grace, the Precious Blood of Christ poured upon our souls,—all through the operation of the Holy Ghost.

Mourning again makes us more Christ-like, for it makes us more like the Man of Sorrows, whose life here was one long life of mourning, and then it drives us to Him for consolation, and then, blessed thought, it makes us partakers of His very Passion. For St. Paul dares to say that he rejoices in his sufferings, and fills up that which is behind of the afflictions of Christ.

Yes, we should think of all sorrow as the necessary and natural result of sin, of our Lord's Passion as the full perfect and sufficient satisfaction for the sins of the whole world, yet leaving to each of us in the sorrows of life, some drops of His Cup to drain, some share of His Cross to bear after Him. And as we strive to bear a sorrow bravely, to endure a disappointment without complaining in the spirit of penitence, with the feeling, "*We receive the due reward of our deeds,*" we may humbly but thankfully rejoice with St. Paul that we are permitted the blessed privilege of filling up what is behind of the afflictions of Christ.

We must not however forget, perhaps the most important use of sorrow, its power of developing the human soul. I fear that were even the best of us to be preserved from all sorrow through life we should become so utterly selfish that our souls would be dwarfed and ruined. Even with the bitter sorrows of life and with all the helps of religion how hard it is to be unselfish, what an undue proportion of our time, and of our strength is engrossed with thoughts of ourselves.

Take away all sorrow, all pain, leave but the trifling existence of a life of mere excitement, and we should soon become so selfish that we should be unendurable even to ourselves. Sorrow helps to kill selfishness, and when our Lord laid down as the universal law of His Kingdom, "*If any man will come after Me let him deny himself, and take up his cross daily, and follow Me.*" It was not because He loved to see suffering, it was not because of any arbitrary efficacy in suffering, but because He knew what was in man, and therefore saw that the root of all our sins was selfishness, and that the only way to conquer that selfishness was by voluntary self-denial and cross-bearing.

One of the greatest of American novelists in his well known work, the Marble Faun, draws the character of Donatello so like an ordinary person of every day life, bright and gay and free from sorrow, but with no lofty views basking like a bird in the sunshine,—until that one crime, committed at another's instigation, and in a moment of passion, embitters the whole life, but in its bitterness develops the soul which before had seemed wanting. And as the months roll by sorrow stamps itself deeper and deeper on Donatello and a gloom gathers around him, but the sorrow has its humanising influence, and when he voluntarily expiates his sin by giving himself up to justice, he is a better and more hopeful man than before.

How often a great sin even, if truly repented, has mellowed and deepened a nature that would otherwise have been but selfish. Then too, none are so strong as the truly penitent, the great difference between Innocence and Sanctity is that Innocence is an untried virtue, Sanctity the virtue which has conquered in the trial. Sanctity has been through the furnace, fought on the battlefield, is disfigured perhaps by many a scar, but has the glory of the victor.

I remember once hearing the two virtues described thus,—picture a father coming home from work at night, his little child, watching for his step, rushes down the stairs, and throws her arms around his neck, it is the meeting of

Sanctity and Innocence! The working man who has suffered and has sinned, but by the grace of GOD has learned to resist and to conquer his sins, and the little child as yet ignorant of sin, and untried in the battle with temptation. Innocence knows not yet the need of penitence, Sanctity has experienced its power.

"*Blessed are they that mourn : for they shall be comforted*," and in the derivation of that word comforted, we are promised what penitence gives—strength, and being strengthened ourselves, we shall be able to help and strengthen others; for no one has such power to help others as the true penitent, no one has such sympathy as he who has sinned and repented, and conquered his sin. It is little help to a weak tempted man to say, I have the same temptations as yours, and I generally yield to them, but oh, what help to be able to say, I once knew the force of those temptations, but by the grace of GOD I have learned to conquer them, and so can you.

We must bear in mind, too, that nothing can be clearer than the teaching of the Scriptures, that all sorrow rightly borne, has in it the element of some future joy. "*He that sows in tears shall reap in joy.*" "*Your sorrow shall be turned into joy.*" "*God shall wipe away all tears from their eyes.*" How sad to have no tears for GOD to wipe away, never to have sown in tears, and therefore to have no harvest of joy. All sorrow that is borne in the spirit of penitence is, so to say, the raw material which is to be turned into the joy of eternity.

Well then may our Lord say these words, "*Blessed are they that mourn: for they shall be comforted.*" He does not say, as the world, Blessed are they who have no sorrows, whose lives are one long sunshine, one great success. No, He knows life too well for that, but "*Blessed are they that mourn,*" they who leave this world, recognising its disappointments and sorrows; "*for they shall be comforted,*"—here in many ways by the Holy Ghost, the Comforter, by being made more Christ-like by suffering, by having through suffering the great faculties of the soul developed, by being made strong through penitence, and so able to strengthen others, and by laying up in the treasure-house of heaven the seeds of a harvest of future joy.

This is but the reward of mourning in this world, and in the world to come, on the shores of eternity, in that great morning when we shall see Jesus standing upon the shore. When we shall hear Him from His great white throne, saying, "Come, ye blessed of My Father, inherit the Kingdom prepared for you from the foundation of the world," then, when all is made clear in the light of His Presence, then shall we be indeed comforted in the knowledge that, to that Kingdom there is no way but through much tribulation, and that our nearness to Jesus then upon the throne of His glory, must depend upon our nearness to Him in time upon the Cross of His shame, then indeed shall we see the blessing of mourning; then shall we for ever experience the happiness of this comfort.

THIRD BEATITUDE.

"*Blessed are the meek: for they shall inherit the earth.*"

The soul, having learned from the two preceding beatitudes its true attitude to GOD and to itself, is now taught its relationship to its fellow man. Meekness is that passive virtue, corresponding to, and forming the foundation for those active works of mercy by which we attain to the perfect fulfilment of our duty to our neighbour.

Every race has its national sins—ours is undoubtedly, pride; so that there is perhaps scarcely any virtue so difficult to acquire, and yet so necessary for the Anglo Saxon race, as meekness.

But at the outset, let us understand clearly what we mean by meekness. This is important because there are few virtues which have so many counterfeits. Perhaps the best way will be to expose these counterfeits, to point out clearly what we do not mean to include under this word.

There is that false meekness which is simply cowardice—pusillanimity, the meekness of a little soul. There is that which is but the outcome of sloth,—then there is the so-called meekness of an easy going disposition, which does not want the trouble of asserting itself. And the meekness of a weak character, which yields to every influence that is brought to bear on it; and again the meekness of the man who has so little conviction of truth, so little principle, that he cares not to contend for the truth, and lastly there is the meekness of the character, which neglects to show a holy indignation at sin. Our Lord promises no blessing to any of these, they are but counterfeits of that meekness, which is to inherit the earth.

In what sort of a man should we look for the true virtue of meekness. Without the slightest hesitation, I answer, true meekness is the mark of a really strong character; for it implies the virtues of self-restraint and moral courage; to study it, we must turn to the lives of truly great men, for example, the Bible says that the man Moses was very meek, and students of history will agree at once that the character and work of Moses towers in solitary grandeur, not merely amongst the men of his own age, but perhaps of the whole ancient world. Those who have carefully studied the influence of the Jews, as a people, on humanity, and who see that under GOD the very character of Judaism was moulded and formed by Moses, would probably admit that with the exception of our Lord and Saviour Jesus Christ, there never has been born on earth any man, the influence of whose character has been more wide-reaching than Moses the meekest of men. But that we may see how far removed is meekness from cowardice, or weakness, or an easy going slothful disposition, let us briefly trace the development of the virtue in the life of Moses.

There can be little doubt that, like St. John the Divine, Moses was of a Choleric temperament, and that his besetting sin was anger—on his first appearance, as a man of forty years of age, the virtue in which he was most lacking was meekness. Moses was a patriot, and when he saw an Egyptian smiting one of his own countrymen, he slew the Egyptian and then perhaps first felt the patriotic mission to deliver his enslaved brethren, he felt the call himself and "*supposed his brethren would have understood how that God by his hand would deliver them, but they understood not,*" and the next day when he found two Hebrews striving with one another, and tried to reconcile them, he was met by the contemptuous question, "*Who made thee a ruler and a judge over us?*" Then Moses fled into the land of Midian, where for forty years he was occupied in the quiet life of a shepherd. What a training; what a trial for a man of his temperament! Brooding over the wrongs of his oppressed countrymen, with the burning spirit of the man of action, eager to strike a blow for their deliverance, and to have to wait, and wait forty long years; but this time was not wasted. No, GOD was training Moses for his great work. He must first learn to conquer himself before he can rule the rebellious Israelites. He must learn self-control, meekness, and then when GOD at length appeared to him in the burning bush, and told him the time for which he had waited so long was come, and he was to deliver Israel, how different is his action! He who had been so impetuous, now shrinks back; he who had been self-confident, now distrusts himself, he had learned those two virtues, self-control, and self-distrust.

He was not perhaps yet perfectly meek, and in all that splendid history of one man by his own force and genius, relying on GOD's help, leading a nation of broken down slaves out of captivity, and making them conquerors of a new world, through all those years of wandering in the wilderness we may see GOD training Moses in that perfect self-control, which made him the very pattern of meekness. Six hundred thousand grumbling, undisciplined, ungrateful Israelites to rule and guide for forty years. We see one outburst of the besetting sin, when he struck the rock, followed by the sad punishment, never to enter the promised land, and Moses passes from our sight the splendid example of the man, who in the power of meekness ruled —nay almost created—in some respects the greatest nation the world has ever seen. And if we turn from Moses to other great heroes, who by their force of character influenced and moulded their fellow men, we shall generally find as one of the most marked characteristics of leaders of men the virtue of self-control, of meekness. So we learn that meekness in its highest perfection is possible only in really strong characters. We read in ancient history of one great conqueror, who wept because he had conquered the world, and there was nothing left to conquer, he did not know all the glory of this virtue, he did not try that which is greater than to conquer the world—to conquer self.

Each of us has within us a microcosm, a little world, and the work to which this beatitude calls us is to conquer that world within us.

We have used many times the word "*virtue*," let me remind you of its true force, it is not mere absence of temptation, not the mere negative innocence of one who has never been tried, but derived from the word, "vis," force, violence, surely it implies that which is developed in us by resistance to temptation, it tells of victory on the world's battlefield. So that meekness of which our Lord speaks is not the mere amiability of a weak character, but the self-control of a truly strong one.

All these Christian virtues come from the realisation of certain truths. Poverty of spirit, humility, is simply the recognition of the truth as to our relation to GOD. Mourning is the result of seeing clearly the truth as to sin and sorrow in the world around us. Meekness is the perception of the truth as to others, a recognition of their rights, of their difficulties, and of the important fact that we are intended to be a discipline to each other. How often as we look into our own life, do we not feel that we have been harshly judged or misunderstood, our motives misinterpreted? Meekness helps us to remember that it is probably so with others. What a wonderful example of this is our Lord's first saying on the Cross, "*Father forgive them; for they know not what they do*." What had they not done? Crucified their best friend, rejected and denied their Lord and their GOD! and in the spirit of meekness, in the exercise of that wondrous self-control, even in His Agony our Lord says, "*they know not what they do.*" What a charitable judgment! Others irritate and wound us; instead of thinking they do it on purpose, let us try and feel perhaps they know not what they do. And then again this virtue will help us to realize that we are doubtless a great trial to others, that without meaning it, without perhaps knowing it, even when doing what seems to be clearly our duty, we may be a great source of annoyance to others. Meekness is thus the recognition of the truth as to the rights and difficulties of our neighbour in his relation to ourself.

A question which should be met here. Is not meekness sometimes a mistake? Are there not times when it is right to be angry, when social justice demands it, and when meekness becomes almost a sin against justice. The answer is surely very simple—be as angry as you please at sin, but do not be angry with the sinner; let your indignation blaze forth at that sin in yourself and others which crucified our Lord, and brought all the sorrows of life into this world, but after the example of our Lord distinguish between sin and the sinner. We read that our Lord in the synagogue, "*looked round about on them with anger, being grieved for the hardness of their hearts,"* but we also have just been reminded that when they had done their worst and crucified Him, He prayed for them, "*Father forgive them.*"

But what is the sphere in which we may best practice this virtue of meekness?

In our work for GOD. We are in such a hurry for success, not only in our schemes for worldly ambition, but quite as much in our schemes for GOD's glory—nay more so; for in worldly matters many a man is contented to work on for years with little result, looking to some far future return for all his labours, but in spiritual matters, how many of us, if when we begin to pray we do not see the immediate answer to our prayer, if when we begin to repent we do not find ourselves at once free from our sins, are discouraged, as though some strange thing had happened to us. Let us remember then in work for GOD that GOD generally disciplines the instrument before using it. We have seen this in the case of Moses, we may trace it in almost every saint whom GOD has called to any great work for Him—take St. John, the great type of the Choleric temperament, the Son of thunder, who wished to call down fire from heaven on that village of the Samaritans that would not receive Christ. Where was he in the long years after our Lord's Ascension, when those tremendous controversies between Judaism and Catholic Christianity, in which St. Paul took so prominent a part, were shaking the new-born Church to its very foundation, when those two parties, which went under the names of the two great teachers, St. Paul and St. James, were striving with intense earnestness, on the one side to narrow down Christianity to being a mere reformed school of Judaism, or on the other to extend it to what it now is, the Holy Catholic Church throughout the world. Where was St. John? That figure which we should have expected to see moving about with fiery impetuosity in the very van of the Church's warriors. Where was He? Like Moses in the wilderness of Midian, so St. John in the solitude of those years which succeeded our Lord's Ascension, waited and learned the spirit of meekness, waited caring for his precious legacy, his Lord's Mother, and preparing for that one work so supremely effective because done in the spirit of self-control,—the Gospel and the Epistles which bear His name, which portray to us, not merely the features of the human character of our Blessed Lord, but which call us with eagle-eye to gaze even upon the mystery of His GODHEAD. Learn from St. John meekness in work for GOD.

Then in our judgment of our neighbour, what a sphere for the daily exercise of the virtue of meekness !

But we must consider the reward : "*They shall inherit the earth*," that is, come into possession of it, rule it in the power of meekness.

So unexpected, is it not ? for the meek, like the weak, are just the ones we should think would go to the wall, but turn to the pages of history, and you will find our Lord's promise abundantly fulfilled, that it is those who have conquered themselves, who conquer others. Those who have learned self-control, who become rulers among men.

And the meek, too, possess the earth without strife, because recognising the rights of others they respect them. Every one is glad when the violent self-asserting man is put down, but the meek, the gentle, the modest, all rejoice in his exaltation.

And here, as in all the beatitudes, we may turn to the example of Christ Himself, for He says, "*Take my yoke upon you, and learn of Me ; for I am meek and lowly in heart : and ye shall find rest unto your souls.*" Think of His self-control—the insults of men, the contradiction of sinners against Himself, the buffet in the face and the meek question, "*Why smitest thou Me ?*"

And then lastly, meekness is the safe-guard against future falls. Why did I fall into that temptation ? From lack of self-control is almost always the answer we must give to ourselves.

"Happy are the meek," yes, happy in themselves, and bringing happiness to those around them. Bringing happiness into this world of mourning—mourning for the world's sins, but not adding to those sins by their unrestrained passions, but in the spirit of self-control helping to check those sins, "Happy are the meek, for they shall inherit the earth."

THE FOURTH BEATITUDE.

"*Blessed are they that hunger and thirst after righteousness; for they shall be filled.*"

This beatitude occupies a most peculiar and important position in this chain of blessings. Strictly speaking there are only seven beatitudes, and this therefore is the central one, separating the three beatitudes which tell of the passive laws of happiness from those three higher laws, which point to the active outcome of the passive virtues. This is indeed, so to speak, the balance in the scales of sanctity, the result and test of the first three laws, the connecting link between the active and passive virtues of christian life.

"*Blessed are they that hunger and thirst after righteousness.*" Let us see how this is but a result and test of the right fulfilment of our duties to GOD, ourself and our neighbour.

Health—physical health—is a sign and indeed

a result of harmonious relations between the various organs of the body, a proof that each is fulfilling its proper function, and this health is generally manifested by a hearty appetite for food. And so with spiritual hunger—it is a sign that right relationships exist between the various faculties of the spiritual life, a mark that the different functions of our spiritual organs are rightly fulfilled. Loss of appetite in the physical life is a mark of disordered relationship between some organs, or perhaps that some one organ is not performing rightly its functions, and so interfering with the regular working of other organs. So, if we do not hunger and thirst after GOD, it is a sign of something wrong or disturbed in one of the relationships of our spiritual life, now there are but three such relationships,—to GOD, to self, to our neighbour. They have been treated in the first three beatitudes, and if we do not hunger and thirst after righteousness, if we do not desire the things of GOD, it is a proof that there is something wrong in one of these relations, that we are failing in our duty either to GOD, ourself or our neighbour, that we have not perfectly learned to be poor in spirit, and to mourn, and to be meek—that pride coming between us and GOD has given us wrong and perverted ideas of our relation to Him, or imperfect penitence in our own lives has blurred our clearness of sight in regard to ourself, or anger or envy has disturbed the harmony of our relation to our neighbour. In a word, if we do not hunger and thirst after righteousness it is because we have not rightly fulfilled our threefold duty.

There is not, I am sure, anything in the whole spiritual life which we so much crave for, and at the same time have to admit that we so little realise, as this longing for the things of GOD, this hungering and thirsting after righteousness.

In the first blush of our conversion from sin, in those moments of ecstasy which spiritual writers have termed the first fervors of the soul, we felt, born within us, a love so different from everything we ever experienced before, a love so absorbing that it seemed to transform our whole life, a love so glorious, so bright that it seemed to turn all the cold and darkness of the world around us into warmth and light. But as life went on that love—instead of burning up brighter and brighter, as we expected, until it had kindled our whole nature—began to wane and fade and grow cold, until with many of us, if we are honest with ourselves, we have to confess to-day that we are not as earnest in our service of GOD, not nearly as warm in our love for GOD, as we were when we made our first Confession, or received our first Communion. Ah, my brother, you may say to me I desire to hunger and thirst after righteousness, I read the lives of the saints who have so hungered and thirsted, and have been filled and satisfied, and I long to make their experience my own, but I do not know how to do it. I try to pray, but prayers become more and more distracted, I come to Communion but that does not seem to help me, I read my Bible, but after awhile only as an irksome duty. Why is it, when our Lord has pronounced such a blessing on those who hunger and thirst after righteousness, why is it, when I long so to have that blessing, that I cannot make it my own?

My brother, the answer is very simple and, it seems to me, very logical and clear. There is something wrong in one of the three preliminary steps, you would hunger and thirst after righteousness if you had learned to be poor in spirit, to mourn, and to be meek, but the beatitudes are not strung together in any arbitrary order, they follow one another in necessary sequence, and you cannot skip any single step, you cannot pass a step higher until you have learned and made your own the lower law; and so in the very centre of the chain there is a halting stage, this—"*Blessed are they that hunger and thirst after righteousness.*" If you have this hunger, if you can appropriate this blessing, it is a proof that the lower laws are learned, the passive duties fulfilled, and a voice which says, "*Friend go up higher,*" invites you into the higher region of an active Christlike life. But if your conscience says you have it not—that you long to have it, but long in vain, it is a sign that something is wrong, and you must go back and begin again.

How important then is this beatitude, testing as it does, all the past, ushering us into the paths of the highest virtues of the Christian life. How many make the mistake of taking the highest seats, when they are bidden at the outset of their spiritual life, of trying to practice the highest virtues of sanctity, only to find the spiritual life crumble from under them, because it has no solid foundation. Ah, my brethren, test yourselves by this law. Do you hunger and thirst after righteousness? If so, thank GOD, and press onward. If not, thank GOD for revealing the truth to you, and go back humbly into the lowest chamber of penitence, until you have found the cause in some unrepented, unconquered sin against your duty to GOD, yourself or your neighbour.

But what is this righteousness, for which we are to hunger and thirst? In a word, Is it not Christ Himself, "*The Lord, our Righteousness?*" First, Christ's righteousness imparted to us through the Sacraments of grace, and then through our co-operation with that grace in the habitual practice of Christian virtue, the righteousness of a saintly, of a Christ-like life.

Hunger enables us to assimilate food to our bodies by which every part is nourished and strengthened. And so hungering for Christ will lead us so to feed upon His Body, so to frequent the Sacrament of the Altar, that instead of taking Christ into every part of our nature, He will take every part of our nature into Him. Sanctifying us wholly in body, soul and spirit, until at last, as St. Paul ventures to say, we have the mind of Christ. His presence in our soul so ruling us that every thought is brought into captivity to Christ. And then the thirst—just as hunger seems to tell of our need to feed more and more upon Christ's Body; so thirst, which, though in a less degree, yet refreshes and nourishes life, speaks to us of a desire to work for Him, for His Body the Church, for those souls for whom He died. It carries us in thought to that supreme moment on the Cross, when the crisis of His Agony, having passed, He uttered the words, "*I thirst.*" From that watch-tower as He looked out into the far future, He saw all those souls, for whom He came to die, souls treading the path which leads but to ruin, souls that even then were steeling their hearts against Him, and in the full passion of His love for them He cried, "I thirst!" telling of His mystical thirst for souls. So if we have this thirst for Christ, it will lead us on to a Christ-like work, to a recognition that no joy can be greater than to be permitted to help to bring a soul to Christ.

But this hunger and thirst after righteousness tells of the true end of our life.—Perfection—to reproduce in ourselves the features of Christ's life, to follow His example, as He said in this same Sermon on the Mount, "*Be ye therefore perfect even as your Father which is in heaven is perfect.*" Perfection! but what is perfection? and is it possible in a mere finite creature like man? Christ does not require impossibilities, and He has said, "*Be ye perfect.*" Now all perfection in creatures is relative. It is the perfect fulfilment of the purpose for which they were created. When GOD created us He had a purpose for each of us, a work for us to do, a certain standard of perfection for us to reach, and when this purpose is fulfilled, when our work is acccomplished, when that standard is reached, that is for us, perfection. It involves much, but it does not require anything which is beyond our powers. It calls for the development of all our faculties, for the attainment of the highest standard we can reach, and this hunger and thirst after righteousness, this desire for perfection, should be, must be the Ruling Passion of our life. What a help it is to have an object in life! if that object be a worthy one, how it ennobles the whole life! Even in mere worldly life a ruling passion an object, a goal, how it transforms a man for good or evil! how it directs and moulds all the course of his life, enabling him to bear up under disappointment, cheering him when discouraged, spurring him on to greater efforts when difficulties arise! How it casts a halo of brightness over the most uninteresting work, and when that ruling passion is the noblest a man can conceive, when that good is heaven itself, the influence it exercises over that man who is its willing slave is indeed glorious.

We complain that religion after a time become tedious, the exercises of spiritual life, dull and tiresome, but if we have this desire for perfection, as the passion of our lives, then what an object of intense and ever increasing interest our religion becomes; but how terrible is the void without it. This desire for perfection is the great remedy for sin; for as in some cutaneous diseases, an irruption on the skin is not cured by mere local application, which would but drive the poison into the system, that poison to which the irruption points, but by strengthening the system. So sin is not to be conquered merely by mere local watchfulness against separate acts and temptations, but how much more by development of life and strength from within, by building up the enfeebled constitution, and so throwing off the disease in the vigor of a healthier life.

It is, too, the great incentive to holiness. Every day to have as the supreme interest of the day, the desire for perfection, the attempt to copy on the canvas of our souls, some features of the character of Christ.

Ah! if our religious life is not what we once thought it would be, if our prayers are distracted, and our hearts cold, and our thoughts taken up with the world, and if religious things are losing their hold on us, their interest for us, is it not because we are contented to take a lower standard than the very best we can do? Is it not that we are not striving after perfection? But after something far below it, which seems easier of attainment, but really is not? Strive after perfection and you shall be made perfect in the struggle, in spite of the many defeats and failures of which you are so painfully conscious. But be contented with something less than perfection, and you will fall back again and again till that love, which must be the source of all religious life, expires within you, and your religion becomes a mere cold corpse of a religion, the soul of which has fled.

Is life worth living? some have asked. To those who have no ambition beyond the grave, the answer may perhaps be, No; but to those who have as the ruling passion, as the supreme interest of their lives, the struggle to be perfect, for them life is worth living, even for the joy it brings in this struggle, and how much more for the great reward in heaven.

Never be satisfied with what you are, or with what you have done; take St. Paul's words for your motto: "*This one thing I do, forgetting those things which are behind, and reaching forth unto those things which are before. I press toward the mark for the prize of the high calling of God in Christ Jesus.*"

"*Blessed are they that hunger and thirst after righteousness.*" There are three times in life when hunger is a good sign. The time of convalescence, when we are recovering from severe sickness; then too, when as children we are growing very fast, and again when we are engaged in very laborious work. So is it in spiritual life. When you are convalescing, recovering from the disease of sin, after, perhaps, your first real act of repentence, you will have a great longing for GOD. Then too, when you are growing very fast in the knowledge and love of GOD this hunger and thirst after righteousness will be a sign of that growth. And so again, when you are working very earnestly for GOD, you will feel the need of very frequent Communion, you will hunger for Christ, that you may give Him in your work to those you have come to love for His sake.

In that beautiful parable of the "Friend at Midnight," which is too often passed over in our Bible studies, when the man goes to his friend at midnight, and asks for the loan of three loaves, what is his plea? "*For a friend of mine in his journey is come to me and I have nothing to set before him.*" The plea is twofold, first a desire to help others, to feed the hungry, to work for GOD. And then a realisation of our own utter poverty, and that all our work must be done in the grace and strength we get from GOD in the Sacraments of His love. And notice, the loaves are asked for only as a loan, so a return must be made, the grace given must be used for GOD's glory, the talent must be multiplied, there must be a sense of responsibility.

But what is the reward? "*Blessed are they that hunger and thirst after righteousness; for they shall be filled.*"

The result of learning the lessons of the first two beatitudes was the emptying the soul of self and sin, now room having been made for Him, it is to be filled with Christ. Christ and self, Christ and sin, can no more wield a divided sway over your soul, than cold and heat can co-exist at the same time and in the same place. But having begun by emptying your soul of self, and then in penitence mourned for sin, and then cultivated that self-control or meekness, by which sin may be kept out of your soul, it is to be filled with Christ.

Hungering and thirsting for Him and in

every Communion finding an ever increasing nearness to Him, and an ever truer possession of Him, this is the reward on earth! but its consummation is in heaven, where we pass into the kingdom of His love, and are indeed filled with Him.

FIFTH BEATITUDE.

"*Blessed are the merciful: for they shall obtain mercy.*"

As soon as we have learned to long after Christ we shall strive to be like Him, and so naturally the next three beatitudes give us the active virtues of a Christlike life.

And these three active or positive laws of sanctity correspond inversely with the passive or negative laws, which we have already considered. Thus Mercy is the active side of meekness. Purity of heart is the positive virtue corresponding to the negative law of penitence, while Peacemaking is the active practice of that duty to GOD, the passive side of which we learned from the first beatitude under the law of poverty of spirit.

In the first three beatitudes we were taught the right attitude, the true relationship, in which we must stand to GOD, ourself and our neighbour, in the three which we are now to consider, having made sure that the relationship is right, we are taught the positive duties which belong to those relationships, the active work we must do in fulfilling those duties. But we cannot pass to these except through that fourth and test beatitude, that is, all the active work in cultivating a Christ-like nature must be done in hunger and thirst after righteousness.

Mercy comes first because it was the first manifestation of GOD's love to man. Creation was an act of mercy, the overflow of GOD's love upon His creatures, which called them into being. The Incarnation was the supreme act of Mercy, when GOD came into that Humanity which He had made to share its sorrows, to heal its sins, to lift it up to His very throne. And then the life of Christ on earth was essentially the life of mercy.

But at the start in considering this quality we are met by a difficulty, one which has puzzled many a mind. How are we to reconcile the Divine Mercy with Divine Justice, and what is the relation which exists between them? On the one hand GOD is all Merciful, on the other hand

He is all Just. In His revelation He has again and again in the most tender and touching way assured us of His mercy for sinners, yet He has no less clearly warned us that all unrepented sin must be punished.

May we not as a preliminary step in clearing the ground point out that mercy and justice are but two different views of a truth. Justice is the viewing of things absolutely as they are, while mercy is the recognition of inherent though latent possibilities in a thing with regard to its future. Thus the judgment of which we read in the twenty-fifth chapter of St. Matthew, by which the goats were eternally separated from the sheep, did not make them either sheep or goats, but simply recognised what they had made themselves, and what they were at a time when there was no further possibility of change. While on the other hand the Divine Mercy and indeed all mercy is the willingness to see possibilities of good in a character already tending far towards evil. Mercy is the looking into a heart which seems so hard and evil, and seeing in it a germ, a spark, of something better, which, though it may require years of effort, may yet be developed, and fanned into a flame; seeing this, and therefore treating it with mercy. But where we best see the reconciliation of the paradox is in our Blessed Lord's Atonement. We turn to the Cross of Christ, and there we see the solution of many of the world's perplexities. At the time of our Lord's life on earth these two great ideas had crystallised in two powerful schools of philosophy, the Epicureans and the Stoics, the one looking on life from the sunny point of view and as, St. Paul tells us, taking for a motto, "*Let us eat and drink and be merry for to-morrow we die.*" These have their representatives, even in our day and among Christians, in those who say GOD is so easy going, and kind, and merciful, He will never allow any one to perish. This class exalt GOD's Mercy at the expense of His Justice and Truth. They were represented among the Jews in our Lord's time by the Sadducees.

Then there was the rival school of the Stoics who marshalled under their banner so many famous names, so many noble natures. They saw the bitterness and disappointment of the world, looked upon life as a hard, stern thing, and tried to crush out love and mercy from their hearts as indications of weakness. In Christianity they find their representatives in the followers of Calvin in the stern doctrines of such election as denies the freedom of the will—in our Lord's time among the Jews the Pharisees were the exponents of their theories. But standing between the two schools, recognising what is true in each, and reconciling their difficulties, we see the Cross of Christ. On the one hand the Passion of Christ witnesses to the malice of sin, to GOD's view of sin, to what sin essentially is. How hard it is for the best of us to realise the sinfulness of sin. We live in an atmosphere tainted with sin. We see it and hear it all around us until familiarity with it blinds us to its horror.

So GOD in forgiving sin chose a way in which the wickedness of sin might be for ever forced on our notice. If GOD, by a mere arbitrary act of His will, had forgiven the sin of the world, man would have been in the greatest danger of losing all realisation of the awfulness of sin, but GOD chose a means for its forgiveness, and in the Passion of Christ, paints with hideous vividness an ineffaceable picture of what sin is, of what sin does. It is the one supreme evil—and it crucifies the Son of GOD. This is what the Passion teaches the Epicurean, the sadness and responsibility of life, the intense reality of sin, and the absolute Truth and Justice of GOD in punishing sin.

But on the other hand, while the Passion portrays in blackest characters the hatefulness of sin, it also exhibits with no less distinctness, the tender love, the wondrous mercy of GOD. If GOD in the Atonement had only revealed His justice, guilty man might have given up the struggle in despair; but no, the Passion preaches to the Stoic the infinite pity, the never failing mercy of GOD. Many of you are familiar with that story of the early days of Greek History, the story of Zaleucus, King of Locri, so famed as a legislator for his severity and impartial justice. How, when his son had committed a crime the punishment for which was the loss of the two eyes, the people wondered what Zaleucus would do—if he exacted the penalty, they would say what a just ruler, but what an unnatural, pitiless father, if he remitted the penalty, they would say he is a tender father, but what an unjust judge. Zaleucus called the executioner and bade him put out one of his son's eyes, then descending from his throne ordered him to put out one of the king's eyes; so that whenever that son looked upon his father, blinded in one eye for his misdoings, he would be reminded of two things—how dreadful it was to offend against the law, since both he and his father had lost an eye to pay the penalty of one crime—how great was the king's love of his son since he was willing to share so terrible a punishment. So as we look at the Cross of Christ we are ever reminded of the awful nature of sin and the strict Justice of GOD, who spared not His own Son, but we also see how He loved the sinner for whom Christ was willing to suffer so terrible a death. So mercy sees good beneath the evil in man, and by its self-sacrifice shows the infinite price it sets upon a human soul.

Is it not the great difficulty in life to believe in man enough? We have been so often deceived, have suffered so many times for our trust, that we begin to lose all faith in human nature. And yet is it not equally true, that by mercy we draw out all the good in human nature? for mercy draws out the very virtue it exhibits. The Cynic is the man who seems to arouse all that is evil, while the merciful man who is always ready to believe the best of his fellow men, though often deceived, yet often has the blessed privilege of awakening the dormant self-respect, of reviving the dying sparks of goodness in some despairing human soul. By showing a belief that there are still germs of good left, he reveals to the desponding sinner possibilities in himself which he had long thought dead, awakens hope and life, and saves a soul!

But we may exercise mercy not only in our dealings with others, but in our judgments of others. How unmerciful we often are in our thoughts, in our words—does this ever help us or any one else? does it not often do irreparable injury to souls? Try to see the hidden good in others, and to work from the side of sympathy till that good swallows up the evil. What a power is the appreciation of the value of a soul! that which GOD so loved that He died for; it must indeed be of priceless value. Try to feel this; to believe that if we could only strike the right chord, there would be a responsive note in every soul, feeble perhaps at first, but swelling and growing till it burst forth in prayer and praise.

But what is mercy?—for like meekness and all virtues, it has its counterfeits. There is a false mercy which is mere good nature, which gives to the relief of the needy, because it costs too much pain to say, No. On this point a most useful hint is given us by our Lord in a single word in the account of the healing of the Deaf Man with an impediment in his speech, one of the two miracles peculiar to St. Mark. "*And looking up to heaven*, HE SIGHED," a better translation would be, " He groaned." He not only relieved the man's necessity, but He felt and sympathised with the man's misery. All active works of mercy must have this passive side, we must not only do for the needy, but suffer with them. A more dangerous counterfeit, however, is what the world calls Philanthropy, more dangerous because so much more subtle in its imitation of mercy,—in fact distinguishable from the true virtue only by the spirit which prompts it. Philanthropy, as its name implies, has man as its beginning, and man as its end, it springs from love of man, not love of GOD, and when correctly analysed, too often its love of man, is simply love of self.

Sometimes the motive is popularity and the praise of men, sometimes it is some pet scheme or hobby which gives an interesting outlet to surplus energy, and though it may accidentally benefit and relieve the needy and suffering, its spring and motive is just as selfish as the spirit of the man who spends all his money and energies in some hobby, which is merely for the improvement of his estate, or to gain the applause of his fellowmen.

True mercy on the other hand, has its foundation in the love of GOD. What is the first and great commandment of the Law? "*Thou shalt love the Lord thy God with all thy heart, and with all thy soul, and with all thy mind. . . . . And the second is like unto it: thou shalt love thy neighbor as thyself.*" But observe that the second is simply the necessary outcome of the first, and is contained in it. If we love GOD absolutely, we must love our neighbour as we love ourselves; because we recognise that our neighbour is equally with us the object of GOD's love. Hence we see that the difference between mercy and its counterfeit mere philanthropy is not a difference which can always be detected from without, it is a difference of motive, the one springing from the love of GOD, and having GOD as its ultimate end; the other from love of self, and having self as its end. How then, you may say, can I tell one from the other? There is a simple test which in most cases is sufficient. Philanthropy, or good nature, is quite compatible with hating some one individual, or systematically neglecting some clear duty. Mercy is not. We may see an instance of this in the Parable of Dives and Lazarus. The rich man may have been, and very probably was a philanthropist, and yet he is condemned for neglecting to perform a duty of mercy.

Dives was prominent, and popular, and being rich, had very likely contributed like other philanthropists, and perhaps largely, to building synagogues and other public-spirited works; but at his own door there lay an object of charity, whom he ignored and refused, as he passed him daily.

There are many active even in Church work,

who are systematically neglecting their duty at home, pouring their sympathy on the poor and sick, who have no direct claim on them, while they are withholding it from some member of their family, a sister perhaps, a husband or a wife, or even a mother or child, who is craving for it, as Lazarus did for the crumbs which fell so plenteously from the rich man's table. Mercy must have its source in the love of GOD.

"*Thou shalt love thy neighbour as thyself.*"

How many love their neighbours far less than themselves; and some few love their neighbours better than themselves, and neglect the cultivation of their own souls by prayer and meditation, for a life of active work, for what they call perhaps the practical side of Christianity. But our Blessed Lord warns us against this mistake, for He spent thirty years in the development of His own spiritual life at Nazareth, before He began His three year's ministry; and even then, He never allowed His prayers to be crowded out; for how often we read of His spending the night in prayer, or rising a great while before day, when the exigencies of His work prevented Him from giving any time during the day to direct commune with His Father.

"*Blessed are the merciful: for they shall obtain mercy.*" The reward, "*they shall obtain mercy*" is the law of GOD's dealings with man. "*With what measure ye mete, it shall be measured to you again.*" In that great picture of the last Judgment, sketched for us in the twenty-fifth chapter of St. Matthew, this is there the ground of our Lord's Judgment—to those on the left hand the explanation was given,—"*Inasmuch as ye did it* NOT *to one of the least of these, ye did it not to Me ;*" while to those happy ones on the right hand the King said, "*Inasmuch as ye have done it unto one of the least of these my brethren, ye have done it unto Me.*" They had shown mercy, they had obtained mercy. How strict will be that judgment, when the greatest Saint must ask for mercy, and the condition is that he must have been merciful.

Happy then will be the merciful: for they shall obtain mercy.

SIXTH BEATITUDE.

"*Blessed are the pure in heart : for they shall see God.*"

The preceding beatitude has taught us a Christ-like life to the world around us, this tells of a Christ-like life towards the world within us. It is the active fulfilment of that duty to self, the passive side of which was taught us in the second beatitude. Purity of heart is the positive virtue corresponding to and springing from the negative virtue of penitence.

What is this purity of heart? It is not on the one hand the mere absence of sin, which we understand by innocence, nor is it on the other, the mere negative cleansing from sin of penitence; but it is the positive purity of a character, which reflects the image of GOD. For this law tells of the active side of our duty to self, which is to cultivate and restore in us that Divine

Image in which we were created, but which was shattered by the Fall of Man.

Let us not take that view of the total depravity of man after the Fall, which is based neither on reason nor revelation. Much was lost, but not all. GOD's Image in us was marred and disturbed, but not entirely destroyed. Just as a mirror which has flaws in it, reflects, but imperfectly, and sometimes distorts almost ridiculously the image reflected; so was it with man's soul. Before the Fall it was a mirror in which GOD was perfectly reflected, since then the reflection has been blurred and confused, and our highest duty toward self lies in the cultivation of such purity of heart as may restore more and more clearly that power of reflecting GOD's Image.

"*Blessed are the pure in heart,*" observe the word, "cleansed in heart," not "unstained," ($κάθαροι$ not $ἄγνοι$). If our Lord had used that other word, what hope could sin-stained souls have had, but no, the blessing belongs to those who, having stained their robes, have washed them and made them white in the blood of the Lamb.

The purity of penitence is the cleansing away

of defilement, but that is not all, it is but the first step, for after the cleansing away of sin, a vacancy is left in the soul. It is like that man of whom we read in the twelfth chaper of St. Matthew, out of whom the unclean spirit went, but who left himself " EMPTY, *swept and garnished*," and therefore an inviting prey to the evil spirits, who came back in greater force, because they found the house empty. When the soul has been cleansed through Absolution, the work of purity has only just begun.

Here let me remind you of the function of the fourth beatitude, through which, so to speak, each virtue has to pass from its passive state to its active manifestation, and by which that passive aspect is to be tested. The negative side of our duty to self was taught in the beatitude of penitence. "*Blessed are they that mourn*," if that penitence was real, if that mourning was deep enough, the result is an intense hunger and thirst after righteousness. Just as a ravenous appetite is the sure sign of returning health after some sickness; so is a great desire for the things of GOD the best sign, the surest test of the reality of penitence, and the consequent forgiveness of sin and cleansing, which GOD has promised to all who truly repent.

But penitence has only cleansed the canvas of our souls while this desire for righteousness will impel us eagerly and earnestly to begin to paint upon that cleansed canvas, the likeness of Christ. Yes, this active purity of heart is the bringing back to the soul the image of GOD by laborious and patient imitation of Christ. There in the four Gospels, in the record of our Lord's life on earth, we see our perfect Example, our Copy, and our work is to reproduce it in our own lives. Nothing can be done till the canvas is cleansed and prepared, sin must first be repented of and absolved, but for those who have known the blessing of cleansing, there is that further purity of heart which consists in the reproduction of the likeness of Christ in the soul. What a solemnity; what an interest does this thought give to life!—the desire for perfection its ruling passion, and the Example of perfection, its Lord, and, at once the means and end of perfection, the painting on the canvas of our soul's life, the representation of our Lord. Each day when we arise, do we realise that we take the brush in hand. Sometimes—perhaps in Lent—by greater prayer and watchfulness we succeed in tracing in ourselves, some features of the character of Christ, and then again in a few weeks of carelessness we take the brush and paint out and obliterate what took us so long to produce. It is recorded of one of the most famous painters of ancient Greece, that a pupil asked him, "Why are you so long over each of your pictures, when your less celebrated contemporaries produce so many more works than you do?" It is said that he replied, "I paint for eternity." With Zeuxis it was but a vain boast; for while the story remains to us, every work from his brush has long since perished, but it has its lesson for us. If a mere heathen painter could take such pains with his work that his fame might last a little longer in this world, what care, what earnest labour should we not bestow on that great picture of our soul's life, our character, which is indeed to last for eternity? Ah, say sometimes to yourself these words, for weal or woe, in copying the life of Christ or the features of a devil, "I am painting for eternity."

"*Blessed are the pure in heart: for they shall*

see God." The reward here, "they shall see GOD," is partly cause, partly effect, in no sense an arbitrary gift, but a necessary result of the cultivation of purity of heart. It is partly cause; for it is only in proportion as we purify our character that we can see GOD; it is partly effect for it is in so far as we see Him clearly that we become like Him.

We must develop a Christ-like character before we can see GOD, for we can only see Him in proportion as we become godly. In the eighteenth Psalm we read, "*With the holy Thou shalt be Holy, and with a perfect man Thou shalt be Perfect. With the clean Thou shalt be Clean, and with the froward Thou shalt learn (or shew) frowardness.*" What do these words mean? They account for the strange distorted views that some men have of GOD, by telling us that a man's idea of GOD will depend largely on the man's own character. Sometimes, when there have been forest fires near us, the sun appears to us like a blood red ball of fire, we exclaim perhaps, "how red the sun is," and yet we know well that the sun is always the same, and that its red appearance is caused by a change in the condition of the atmosphere through which we view it; and it is exactly so with regard to man's view of GOD, he can only see GOD through the atmosphere of his own character, as reflected in the mirror of his own heart, and hence it is that a holy man has an intense realisation of GOD's Holiness, a man who is earnestly striving after perfection, sees GOD as the Perfect One, to the pure in heart GOD reveals Himself as the Pure One, whilst to the froward and the sinner, GOD, seen through the medium of the atmosphere with which they have surrounded their lives, seems harsh and severe, and even cruel and unjust.

Now we understand why to see GOD is the special blessing of the pure in heart: for it is only the pure in heart who can see Him as He is; and it is the result of their purity of heart that they see Him. Others may have a theoretical belief in the Holiness and Perfection of GOD, but we only realise these attributes in GOD in so far as we are striving after them in ourselves.

But there is yet a step further in the cultivation of this purity of heart. We must remember it is the effort to develop every faculty of our nature ; our character must not only be freed from flaws, it must also be complete ; and thus we see how wonderfully this beatitude gives us all the positive side of our duty to self, how far-reaching are its requirements, to cultivate every faculty of our nature, to copy, to reproduce every feature of Christ's life in us. What must we keep in mind in making this effort? First, the duty of meditation — the spiritual perception must be cultivated in meditation, the ear of the soul trained to catch the whisper of GOD's voice, trained to listen to the very silences of GOD, and then the trained ear teaches the spiritual eye, till at last in meditation that eye contemplates the glories of heaven, pierces the clouds of sin, which hide heaven from us, and gazes upon the thorn-crowned Face of the Beloved of our soul. Happy are the pure in heart : for they shall see GOD.

But meditation is not an easy exercise, and depends largely, not only on the immediate moment of the meditation, but on the general purity of the soul in its daily life. Do not isolate the struggle for purity too much from other struggles. This purity must be something more than mere successful defence, it requires edification, the building up of the whole character. There is a danger with all temptations of becoming so absorbed in watching against some one sin, that we nervously let the very dread of falling into it sometimes become a temptation in itself. Yes, the struggle for purity is to be not so much a striving after one particular virtue, as the effort to build up our whole life after the Pattern of Christ's life; not so much in the continual watching against temptation, as in the becoming so absorbed in contemplation of our Example Christ, that we forget that there is any possibility of our breaking the law of purity. But while I say do not concentrate your attention too much on this virtue, you must not forget that assaults upon it generally begin with little temptations to luxury, and never probably has there been a time in the Christian Church when these temptations to luxury in small things have been so strong and insidious. We need to bear in mind St. Paul's precept to St. Timothy, " *Thou therefore endure hardness as a good soldier of Jesus Christ!*" The customs of the age have created a thousand little comforts and luxuries, which we persuade ourselves are necessary for us, and how often it is these small luxuries which open the gates to many a temptation against purity.

Then when tempted remember not merely that you have grace within you, but that law of grace that it does not manifest itself until it is used. When our Lord in the Synagogue said to the man with the withered hand, "Stretch forth thine hand," He was commanding him to do what seemed to be impossible, for the very fact that the hand was withered implied inability to stretch it forth, but it was in the effort to do what seemed impossible that the grace worked and the hand was restored. So when our Lord commanded the ten lepers to go show themselves to the priests, He was commanding them to do what seemed quite useless; for it was not the priests' work to cleanse the leprosy, only to certify to its cure. But as they went, as they tried to obey, the grace worked, and they were cleansed.

How many deluded souls pray for more grace, and complain they need more grace, when they are not using what they have, with most of us it is not more grace but more will that we need, more effort of our own to co-operate with GOD'S grace; so in temptation remember you must not wait till the grace manifests itself, but begin to resist, and in your resistance the grace will enable you to conquer.

We are now considering what practical helps there are to resist assaults against purity, we must not forget perhaps the most important of all, a cultivation of a spirit of recollection, a continual realisation of GOD's presence. I said just now that the reward "*they shall see God,*" was partly the result of purity of heart, partly the cause of it. Yes, for as the cultivation of purity of heart enables us to see GOD, so does that sight of GOD banish from us all temptations against purity; for how powerless is temptation when we are gazing upon GOD.

And from this thought flows another, the importance of perfect sincerity in our religious life, the care we should take that our inner life be not something different from our outer life. We are reminded too of this by the words "*pure in heart,*" the heart, the inner life, not merely the outer life is to be pure.

It is so easy to wear the garb of religion, to adopt the phraseology of religion, to admire the poetry of religion, and yet for our inner life to be untouched by all this. If we are to be pure in heart we must be transparent in our lives, we must aim at great sincerity.

"*Blessed are the pure in heart: for they shall see God.*"

Such is the reward—no mere arbitrary gift, but a necessary result, an ever growing happiness. As purity is cultivated, so the image of GOD glows and burns in the soul.

This reward is partial now, perfect in eternity. Now to see GOD in all the works of nature, in the glorious sunset, and the majestic mountain which stands out in such grand relief against the sky, in the sweeping curves of the river as it winds like a silver thread through the grateful fields, and pours itself into the bosom of the mighty ocean—to see GOD in His greatest work, Man, hidden perhaps beneath the garments of sin, but still there in every possibility of good yet left, to see GOD in our own nature, oh, what happiness! to trace His image more and more in our own souls, but great as this Blessedness is, it is nothing to that supreme blessedness, which is to be the consummation of all, when "*Thine* eyes shall see the King in His Beauty: they shall behold the land that is very far off." To see Him as He is, and to be like Him! No words can tell then how happy will be the pure in heart: for they shall indeed see GOD.

SEVENTH BEATITUDE.

"*Blessed are the peacemakers: for they shall be called the childred of God.*"

Although we still have left for our consideration one beatitude, which tells us the result, both in this life and in the life to come, of having lived according to these laws of sanctity; yet speaking strictly, we may consider this beatitude, "*Blessed are the peacemakers,*" as the last of the laws of happiness, as teaching us that active duty towards GOD which is the complement of the first Beatitude, and which shows us in all its fulness our true relationship to GOD

"*Blessed are the peacemakers*" for they have reached the topmost round of the ladder of sanctity, the highest stage of a Christ-like life, the very reproduction of our Lord's life upon earth. Christ came into this world not only that He might show mercy to the suffering, not only that He might cultivate one perfect soul, but that He might do His Father's Will, that He might finish His Father's work, that He might win back the world to GOD, and bring to an end the bitter war, and bestow upon weary man, the gift of peace; and so angels in the midnight skies of Bethlehem heralded His Birth with the song, " *On earth* PEACE;" so again, when the battle had been fought and the victory won, after His Resurrection our Lord appeared to His Apostles saying, " PEACE *be unto you.*"

Let us first carefully seek the exact meaning of this word Peacemakers ($\varepsilon i \rho \eta \nu o \pi o i o i$). Some have understood this word as though it were merely equivalent to "the peaceable," and the rendering of the Vulgate (*Pacifici*) supports this view, but this would be but a passive virtue, and would be to leave untranslated half the word. The peaceable would be only $\varepsilon i \rho \eta \nu i \varkappa o i$, but the word here is literally those who work peace, and we find it again, St. James iii. 18. This is something positive, something higher, the active virtue of those, who not merely are peacemakers in the sense of striving to heal quarrels, and to reconcile those who are at variance, but who, looking out upon the world around, and realising that the strife and discord which they see everywhere is alike foreign to GOD's original purpose for the world and for man, set themselves to the work of harmonizing the confusion, at least as far as is in their power.

The peacemakers then are those who realize that their duty to GOD is best fulfilled on its positive side by efforts to carry on the work of Christ in bringing peace into this world—peace into man's own nature, peace between man and his fellow man, peace between man and GOD.

This work of peacemaking is not to be carried on on the one hand by ignoring the condition of strife around us, nor on the other by the surrender of every principle of right and truth, but by looking facts in the face, and by so contending for truth that peace comes as the result of victory. When we turn to our Example, the Prince of Peace, we observe that never to save Himself pain or shame did He in the slightest degree compromise truth. Hence at the outset we see clearly that no blessing is pronounced on the "peace at any price" policy of the coward.

In political economy there is a law that peace is the result of war, or of preparation for war.

There is scarcely a nation in the world now at peace, which cannot say "we fought to win the peace we now enjoy. There were great principles at stake for which our forefathers bled that they might bequeath us, not the peace of spirit-broken slaves, but the peace of freedom."

The peacemakers then, whom our Lord calls blessed, are not those who through cowardice avoid strife for truth's sake, but those who contending bravely for the faith once delivered to the saints, and having won the victory of truth on earth, are able to help towards that great work of peace, which cannot be consummated until the peace of GOD which passeth understanding is realised in that Kingdom of GOD of which we read, "Peace is within her walls and plenteousness within her palaces."

We see the same law in our Lord's life, after His victory on the battlefield of Calvary, His greeting to His Apostles is continually, "*Peace be unto you*," before the battle was fought He tells them in His last discourse, "*In the world ye shall have tribulations, but be of good cheer, I have overcome the world*," then comes the last sharp struggle, and then the gift of peace.

But we observe a second law in the social order connected with this gift of peace—not only is it the result of war but it needs in order to retain it continual preparation for war.

If we look at Europe to-day and ask what is the cause of the harrowing distress that is felt by the poorer classes in almost every country? We may be met with the reply this suffering is largely caused by the tremendous taxation, and a great part of this taxation is necessary in order to support large standing armies, and immense and costly navies.

And these are required, not because these nations wish for war, but because they sigh for peace, but realise that in the day when they allow that armament to go down, in that day the war-cloud will burst over them; so that to preserve peace they must always be prepared for war. This law too has its analogy in the spiritual order. Not only must we win our peace by a real fight with the powers of evil, but if we are to keep that peace we must be always prepared for attacks, watching and ready, if need be, to fight again.

Then there is a third law not so much in regard to peace as to peacemaking. We can never be of any real help to others as peacemakers until we have won the victory over temptation ourselves. Until that time, until we have fought and won our own peace, we can in no real sense appropriate the blessing which our Lord promises to the peacemakers.

In this beatitude we pass out of our own private spiritual life into the work of bringing back the world to GOD, but mark the position of this beatitude! it is the last of the series, it does not come till after "*Blessed are the pure in heart*," it does not come until after we have learned to cultivate our own spiritual life.

I cannot lay too much emphasis on the necessary and logical sequence of these laws of happiness, on the exquisite symmetry with which they are built one on the other; so that we cannot practice any one law till we have learned those which precede it. And so this last beatitude, which tells of the possibility of our sharing in the very work of the Son of GOD, the work of peacemaking, cannot be reached except by passing through all the others, and especially its predecessor; for we must have made some progress in the development of our own spiritual life, we must have become pure in heart so as to see GOD, before we can work for Him. There is perhaps no fallacy so common amongst people as the idea that they can work acceptably for GOD in the world or in the Church before they have done their work for GOD in their own souls; but we must realise our utter inability to help others until GOD has first helped us. Yes, we must have attained to such purity of heart as shall have enabled us to gaze upon GOD before we can go out to tell other people of Him. We learn here one condition of effective preaching—it must not be the description of a mere picture, the rhetoric of mere human eloquence, which while it may interest the mind can never touch the soul of the hearer, but as St. John writes in the beginning of his first Epistle, "*That which we have heard, which we have seen with our eyes, which we have looked upon, and our hands have handled, of the Word of life . . . declare we unto you.*" St. John's power as a preacher, St. John's marvellous thrilling force as a writer, came from the fact that he was not writing a mere essay on something which he had studied, but with words of burning eloquence which came from his very heart, he was depicting that which he had heard and seen, and his very hands had handled of the Word of life, of Christ Himself.

At the risk of repetition let me again warn you that we cannot do GOD'S work really well in the world around us until we have done it earnestly and thoroughly in the world within us.

When GOD first created the world, all was harmony; then came that catastrophe which brought ruin on GOD'S fair creation, a catastrophe probably caused by the fall of the devil and his angels, who in their malice reduced the earth to the state described in the second verse of Genesis, " *And the world was* ' WASTENESS AND DESOLATION *and darkness was upon the face of the deep,*" for we read " *there was war in heaven: Michael and his angels fought against the dragon; and the dragon fought and his angels, and prevailed not; neither was their place found any more in heaven, and the great dragon was cast out, that old serpent, called the Devil and Satan, which deceiveth the whole world: he was cast out into the earth and his angels were cast out with him.*" And thus discord and confusion came into this earth, discord with GOD first when man rebelled against GOD at the Fall, and then followed discord among men when at the Tower of Babel GOD confused men's tongues, and discord in speech came into the world; and so St. Paul in the second chapter of his Epistle to the Ephesians passes from Christ's work in restoring peace among men, to Christ's work in restoring man to peace with GOD.

Let us now consider what we can definitely do to become peacemakers.

In the highest sense peacemaking is of course the work of the priest, in the ministry of penitence, reconciling sinful souls with GOD. There is a tendency in our times to over-rate the importance of preaching—this in as far as it touches the conscience and leads to repentance is a work of peacemaking—but to deal with the individual soul, and through the Sacrament of Penance to make peace in that soul, this is the most Christlike mission of the Christian priesthood.

But there is yet plenty left for the layman to do, the great work of intercession for the conversion of sinners, especially the work of Eucharistic intercession, at the moment when our great Peace-offering is on the Altar, pleading for dying souls, this work ought to form part of the definite rule of every Christian life.

Then thirdly there is missionary work, an ample field! Think of the millions of human souls as Altars upon which the fire of divine love has never yet been kindled, think of the hearts where once it burned, but where now it has died out and grown cold, and remember that all that you can do for the missionary cause by your prayers, by interesting others, by personal work, by your alms, all that you can do towards spreading the Gospel of Christ is earning the blessing of the peacemakers.

But lastly let us turn from that great world which knows not Christ, to the so-called religious world in which we live. Is there not a Babel of sects and opinions here? Sad as it may be to think of the heathen in lands which have not yet been warmed by the Sun of Righteousness, is it not sadder still to see those around us, who, baptised in the same faith as ourselves, still differ in so many points, and so bitterly? I mean, of course, the Babel of Sectarianism. Here surely is need of peacemaking, but how is it to be done?

Much has been written and said about Christian Unity; some would have it by eliminating all that is positive in Christian dogma. Such unity would be worse, far worse, than the present schism. Without venturing to dogmatise on so difficult a question, let me point out one great principle which can hardly fail to be helpful—to be very strong in our affirmation of all that we believe, but very slow and careful in our negation of doctrines. Truth is so many sided, it is impossible for one person to see all round it, and very often those who are bitterly contending about some doctrine, are each of them realising a different side of the same truth, are both right in what they affirm, are both wrong in what they deny, the complete truth being all the affirmative teaching of both sides.

We probably do not realise enough that even among Sectarians their positive faith is generally true. Error comes in because they are not contented with saying, "I believe this and this," but go on so rashly to say, "I deny that and that."

Let us then be very clear and strong in affirming all that is positive in the Christian faith, but let us be very slow to deny anything that has not been clearly proscribed by the Church.

Heresy is generally the exaggeration of a truth, or of one side of a truth, till it is made to contradict or exclude some other truth.

The saddest heresy of all, that which denies the Divinity of our Blessed Lord, is only false when it denies, it is true when it affirms so strongly the beauty of His perfect Humanity.

Pray then for peace, for unity in faith as well as morals, and contribute your little share to the good work by earnestly contending for the faith, but carefully avoiding the putting of stumbling blocks in the way of others by useless denials.

Then to pass from the conflict between schools of theology to that which seems to exist between theological and scientific truth—to the work of peacemaking, of making harmony between Religion and Science. Let us begin by recognising the trite observation that so far as truth is concerned it is absolutely impossible for Scientific and Religious truth to be antagonistic or contradictory. The whole difficulty lies in schools of theology teaching as matters of revelation what are mere theological speculations or opinions, and what are not " de fide," and in schools of science, putting forth as incontestable truths mere scientific guesses, or hypotheses which, while they account for one class of observed facts, are presently contradicted by some further investigations.

In our work of peacemaking, let us be very careful to be accurate in our theological statements, and not to confound the region of absolute revealed truth with that of interesting theological speculation; and instead of looking on science as the enemy of religion, let us welcome and help forward the efforts of conscientious scientists to cast more light upon the perplexities of the problem of life, remembering that there is no truth in revelation which has been declared a truth by the authority of the Chuch which has ever yet been overthrown by any scientific truth, and that the difficulties lies on the one hand in our exalting mere human interpretations of revealed truth, and on the other, in the too hasty generalisations of unscientific men of science.

Seventh Beatitude.

There is yet left, one field for peacemaking that I will touch on, the relations of Christianity to the other great religions of the world, such as those of Buddha and Mahomet. Where some people have found more difficulty in the points of agreement than in the differences. Let us recognise what is good in all—there is no difficulty in a Christian seeing much that is good and beautiful in those old world religions, for St. John himself in his Gospel tells us that Christ is "*The true Light which lighteth* EVERY *man that cometh into the world*," not that He is the Light only of those in His Church, but that all earnest seekers after truth, like Buddha, have lived in friendship not in enmity with Christ.

So realising that the climax of the ladder of sanctity is—to be allowed to take part in the very work of GOD Himself, let us strive to be peacemakers.

And the reward: "*They shall be called the* SONS *of God*." Unfortunately, our translation has *children* of GOD, but it is υἱοί not τέκνα—more than children, Sons, and why? Because peacemaking is the very Office of the Only Begotten Son of GOD, whose title is the Prince of Peace, and we who, after having purified our hearts, are permitted in however small a degree, to share in His work of reconciling the world to GOD, are also permitted to share in this title.

When our work is done, and at the last day we stand in that Kingdom of Peace, toward which we are looking, for which we are longing as we travel on through this world of strife, when we see standing there with us one whom we have helped in his journey there, what joy it will be to hear him say, "it was your words, your work that under GOD first led me to desire to be reconciled to GOD, that led me here!" That will indeed be to enter into the joy of our Lord! then we shall indeed know how happy are the Peacemakers!

EIGHTH BEATITUDE.

"*Blessed are they which are persecuted for righteousness' sake: for their's is the Kingdom of heaven.*"

The seven beatitudes which we have been considering, teach us the virtues of a saintly life. This eighth tells us what will be the result both here and hereafter of practising these virtues.

If we are to mount up to that life of sanctity which our Blessed Lord came into the world to set before us, we must be poor in spirit, and mourn, and be meek; we must hunger and thirst after righteousness, and be merciful, and pure, and peacemakers—and then, when we have attained to the practice of all these, then we must make up our mind to be persecuted here on earth, and Christ promises that the Kingdom of heaven shall be ours in eternity.

As soon as we have, by the exercise of the last beatitude, reached the title of Sons of GOD, we must be ready to share the sufferings of the Only Begotten Son of GOD.

This beatitude—which is not strictly one of the series, inasmuch as it does not tell us of anything that we are to be or to do, but only foretells what we must suffer as the result of being GOD's children—promises no blessing on the mere endurance of suffering, unless that suffering be for righteousness' sake. When we were treating the fourth beatitude, "*Blessed are they which do hunger and thirst after righteousness*," we took the word righteousness as one of the titles of our Lord, and as equivalent to Christ; so here we might transpose the words and read Blessed are they which are persecuted for Christ's sake, that is, whose sufferings are either the direct result of Christ's service, or proceeding from some other cause, become sanctified by being offered up to Christ and borne in union with His sufferings.

There are few indeed born into this world who do not have sooner or later to taste the cup of suffering, but no blessing is here promised to these sufferings, unless the shadow of Christ's Cross falls upon them.

How many there are who suffer. Ah! and suffer so that it makes our heart bleed to think of their sufferings, and yet who lose the blessing which belongs to suffering, because they merely endure with stoical determination, what they cannot avoid, and forget to offer it in a spirit of resignation to their Heavenly Father. And yet all suffering, if borne in reliance on the Holy Ghost, and under His guidance, is a blessing; for it makes us more like the Man of Sorrows.

But why is it that conformity to Christ's teaching must lead to persecution, to suffering? It is surely because a Christ-like life must be a continual witnessing against the world. I mean the so-called Christian world; for since the days of Constantine, when the world took the Church into its embrace, Christendom has only been another name for the world.

In these beatitudes we have Christ's code of morals, and we cannot disguise from ourselves the fact that they are very different from the world's moral code, and indeed, all the beatitudes taken in their fulness, are a more or less complete protest against the world's teachings, and the world will revenge itself by persecuting those who witness against it.

And this is the doctrine of the Cross. When our Lord set forth these beatitudes, He warned us that it was not enough to be poor in spirit, penitent and meek, not enough to do works of mercy and purity and peace, not enough to hunger and thirst after righteousness, but that if we are to be His followers, we must add to this "being" and "doing"—"suffering." If the beatitudes had stopped short at this one, we might have said "they are glorious laws of sanctity, but as a revelation, they are incomplete, for where is the symbol of our salvation; where is that Cross without which we cannot be Christians," it is not left out, and the eighth beatitude is added for the express purpose of warning us that the path of sanctity must always be a path of suffering.

Is it not striking in all our Lord's teaching, the honesty with which, whilst promising splendid rewards beyond the grave, He reminds us that in this life there must be the Cross. Other leaders of men, other founders of religions have put forth in glowing terms, some temporal rewards, but to the man who said, "*Lord, I will follow Thee whithesoever Thou goest,*" Christ replies, "*Foxes have holes and birds of the air have nests; but the Son of Man hath not where to lay His Head.*" He warns him in the midst of his enthusiasm to stop and count the cost, that he cannot be a follower here of the Man of Sorrows without himself becoming acquainted with grief.

There are ever two results of suffering here, it sanctifies or it sours. The suffering in each case may be the same, the difference depends on the spirit in which it is borne. It may develop in us all the glories of sanctity, or it may warp and twist our nature and make us only bitter and sour, and all depends on that one little condition, whether we bear it for Christ's sake or not. Whether, when the hour of trial comes, we look upward with gentleness and love, and strive to say from our heart, "*Propter Te, Domine,*" or whether we merely strive to endure with a stoical fortitude, which finally degenerates into cynical obstinacy.

But what are the sources of this persecution of which our Lord warns His children. The simplest way to arrange them, is perhaps under our three-fold temptations—from the world, the flesh, and the devil,—the assaults which are directed against the carnal, moral, and spiritual, parts into which our human nature is divided.

As to the world, if we have been steadily witnessing against its precepts by our lives, earnestly resisting its temptations, it will revenge itself by bringing on us persecution, and its persecutions generally fall under one of three heads, first ridicule—the world points at you as straight-laced, prudish, eccentric, if the strictness of your life is a reproach to its social tone. Then isolation—to have to stand alone, to be shunned even by friends, it takes a noble soul to stand alone against the world. But there are many such, whom neither ridicule nor the fear of isolation would force to one action which their conscience told them was wrong, who still yield to the world's last threat, poverty. At first sight it would seem as though the fear of mere poverty would be the last thing to break down a will which had stood firm against ridicule and desertion, and for the man who is alone in the world poverty need have few terrors, but it is different with the one who is weighted with family responsibilities, the affectionate husband, the fond father, who in the tremendous competition of business life, finds himself in danger of being left behind, unless he does as others do, and adopts methods of business, which his conscience tells him, are not honorable, scarcely honest, certainly contrary to the spirit of the Gospel. Perhaps he resists for awhile but at last a crisis comes and he has to look ruin in the face, and what does ruin mean, not merely privation and poverty for himself, but for those whom he loves and who are so dependent on him, those daughters whom he has educated to fill with distinction, the place in society, to which they are entitled. To think of them thrown on the mercies of a heartless world, their very culture unfitting them for the struggle for a living in which they must engage. The world points him to two paths and says choose, do as others do, adopt the ways of the world, and don't set yourself up as so much better than others, live by my rules, prosperous and honoured, dispensing your bounty in works of philanthropy—or for righteousness' sake, follow the strict interpretation of the laws of Christ and live in poverty, unable even to help those almost helpless ones who are dependent upon you. The furnace into which the world threatens to cast those who will not bow down with the multitude to the image of Gold, is indeed a very real one. It needs that a man should have thoroughly learned the first beatitude, Blessed are the poor in spirit, those who rejoice in their dependence on GOD, and can trust Him even when the future looks darkest.

Then there are the persecutions of the Flesh: The body which is at once the instrument of our good works and of our sins, the body with its appetites and its weaknesses craving for a little indulgence here, and a little consideration there. Oh, how it persecutes us. We little realize in these days of luxury, how many of our temptations really spring from the persecutions of the flesh. I am not now thinking of any of the grosser ones, but of those little comforts of nineteenth century civilization,—those little necessities of what we are pleased to call a life of culture, which go so far towards undermining all real strength of will and character; little luxuries which our fathers never dreamed of, but which to us have become so a part of our life, that we persuade ourselves it would be impossible to do without them, and all these little concessions enervating the body, so that instead of its being the obedient slave of the will, and promptly carrying out all its behests, it has rebelled so often and so successfully, it has pleaded and gained its point so many times, that it has become the tyrant of the will, dragging down the moral nature into captivity to its appetites. To take but one example, sloth in rising, a temptation of the flesh of course, and yet how much that is wrong through the day, hurried prayers, imperfectly performed duties, may be traced back to the first act of self-indulgence in the morning.

Lastly we have the persecutions of the devil, these, strictly speaking, move in the sphere of our spiritual life, and aim at separating us from GOD, either by sins against faith or worship. They are without doubt the special temptations of our day. Sins against faith—the devil through the spirit of the age, trying to persuade us that it does not matter much what we believe, or indeed, if we believe anything. Sins —against worship—that we can approach GOD with the easy irreverent familiarity which has done so much to undermine religion, and that we may substitute for the Sacraments of His appointment, the mere services of human taste.

That tempter came to our first parents in the garden of Eden, and suggested a doubt as to the truth of GOD's revelation, "*Hath God said, ye shall not eat of every tree of the Garden?*" At first he does not absolutely deny the truth of GOD's words, only suggests a doubt as to whether GOD really meant them, then when that doubt has done its work, he goes on further to positive denial, when he says, "*Ye shall not surely die.*" So in our days he begins by instilling doubts as to the authenticity or meaning of GOD's revelation, and then goes on to a denial of the truth of that revelation; one doctrine after another is assailed, but so insidiously as to make some people think they are doubting and investigating in the interests of truth, instead of in the interest of the father of lies.

But there are many whose faith is too firm to admit of much hope of success for Satan in this direction, and so leaving their faith alone, he directs all his energies to interfering with their worship of GOD. He attacks them through their prayers, haunting them with distracting, distressing thoughts, striving to interpose his suggestions between their souls and the Throne of Grace, and how often he succeeds! How many who have never had any doubts as to GOD's revelation, grow weary of prayer, and gradually give up all earnest effort to worship GOD.

It would be a great gain to some, if they could only realise that much of the difficulty in prayer which they put down to their own sin, is simply this temptation:—if they could only keep steadily before them the conviction that most of our battles are lost or won on our knees, and that instead of expecting the time of prayer to be a time of freedom from temptation we should remember that the very act of prayer is a challenge to Satan, a challenge which he is sure to accept. With many the attempt to pray and to meditate is the very agony of their spiritual lives. Would it not be a help and comfort to such, to remember that it was so with our Lord Himself, for what was that Agony in the garden of Gethsemane, but a struggle in prayer.

Gaze upon Him as He kneels there on the cold, hard ground, in the light of the Paschal moon. It is the last night of His life, and He looks forward to the horrors of the next day. Thronging around Him, haunting Him are what shadowy forms! Not only the tortures of the Cross are before Him, not only the cruel cry "*Crucify Him, crucify Him,*" is ringing in His ears, but all the sins of the world are crowding upon Him, from that first sin of Adam to the last sin which this world shall witness before the Coming of the Day of Judgment,— your sins and my sins in horrid procession they wind before his eyes. He weighs their guilt and takes them upon Himself, and then He strives to pray with all these cares upon Him, with all these sins around Him from which His pure nature shrank in horror even while He willed to bear them, to atone for them; and more, it was, He tells us, the hour of the power of darkness; in some mysterious way the Evil One brought all the force of his temptations

Eighth Beatitude.

upon Him to hinder His prayer. Three times He prayed a short fervent prayer, using the same words, adding to His prayer that act of resignation, "*Nevertheless not my will, but Thine, be done,*" teaching us that in times of great distraction, when we need to pray with great fervency, and when perhaps it is impossible to gather the forces of our mind, and to concentrate them on a long prayer, it is good to use some short ejaculation, and to keep on repeating it, until the temptation has passed away.

So let us endeavour to grasp this law that Prayer is not always to be a joyous Communion with GOD, far more often it is to be an agony, the arena on which we are to wrestle with our great spiritual foe. And what makes the exercises of devotion so difficult is not only that they are the special sphere of Satan's temptations but that these temptations are greatly aggravated by the slothful cravings of that body, which is so often traitorously in league with Satan instead of being the obedient servant of the soul.

"*Blessed are they which are persecuted for righteousness' sake.*" We think perhaps of the days of persecution as belonging only to the first three centuries of the Church's life, or at most as being revived in those bitter persecutions, which tell of very different ideas of civilization to our own, when religious people and Christians strove to compel uniformity of faith and worship by invoking the aid of physical pain and death, but though persecutions for righteousness' sake have entirely changed as to their kind they have not abated in degree and while men are not earnest enough to care to persecute in our day for differences of faith, the world, the flesh and the devil still persecute for righteousness' sake.

Before we pass to the reward promised let us pause a moment to notice some laws which regulate the temptations or persecutions which we suffer for righteousness' sake. St. Paul collects them together in his first Epistle to Corinthians in these words, "*There hath no temptation taken you but such as is common to man: but God is faithful, who will not suffer you to be tempted above that ye are able, but will with the temptation also make a way to escape, that ye may be able to bear it.*"

He reminds us first that our trials are not peculiar. How often we are tempted to think that our temptations or troubles are so much greater than those of others, here we are distinctly told it is not so and it should help us to think that many a Christian has endured and conquered in just such a struggle as we have to face. Why is it that our temptations seem peculiarly hard to us? It is because they are chosen by Satan to press upon the weak spot in our character, and this is allowed by GOD Who knows that this is the only way to strengthen it. Just as a weak limb is made strong by continual use, and special exercises are devised to bring into play those muscles which are weakest, and these at first weary and even pain us but finally end in developing the weak part. So is it with temptation. Satan chooses those parts of our moral nature in which he finds us weakest and brings the whole force of his temptations to bear upon them. GOD over ruling his malice for good knows well that those weak parts must be strengthened and developed by resistance to temptation if we are to be fitted for the kingdom of heaven: so those trials which seem peculiarly hard to us are common to those who have the same natural faults that we have, and are the only means by which those faults can be eradicated.

Then he speaks of a second law that GOD *"will not suffer you to be tempted above that ye are able."*

How full of encouragement is this promise. When we sometimes say my trials, my temptations are too great for me, we are met by these words which assure that they never are greater than our strength; up to the full of your strength, very often requiring you to use all the grace GOD has bestowed on you, but not beyond it. Indeed we may regard temptation as a sort of measure of our grace, for its force is equal to the grace GOD has given us. Just as you measure the weight of a column of air by its pressure on our hand, so may you estimate the amount of grace GOD has bestowed on you by the pressure of temptation, so that very little trial in this world generally means very little grace. And then again temptation is a wonderful help to self knowledge. How little we should know of the weak spots in our character without it. When we have met with an accident the surgeon comes and by the pressure of his hand gives much pain and so reveals the extent of the wound, but that pressure does not cause the bruise, it only reveals its extent. So temptation may be made a great antidote to self deceit as well as an immense factor in the development of our moral nature; and that moral nature must be cultivated that we may have the capacity to enjoy that kingdom of heaven which is our inheritance. Imagine a person utterly uneducated and without a single cultured taste coming into an immense fortune, what is he likely to do with it? enjoy it he cannot; and so he probably spends it in ministering to some low and degrading passion. Imagine a soul ushered into eternity without the capacity for enjoying any of those things which GOD has prepared for them that love Him. Heaven would be no place of bliss for them. So as we pass through the furnace of temptation and feel all the force of persecution for righteousness' sake pressing upon us, let us recollect that these things are moulding and developing our character, that on them depends much of the joy in eternity. St.

Ephrem Syrus represents GOD as the great Potter, first moulding the clay in our creation, and then placing us in the furnace of temptation and trial in this world, and watching us with loving Providence, exposing us to just enough heat to perfect us,—a little less trial and the vessel would be soft and useless, a little more than it can bear, and it would be cracked and spoiled. And He not only tempers the heat, but orders the duration of the temptation. We pray that a trial may be taken from us, pray in our blindness, and GOD in His love leaves it till it has done its work. There are few aspects of GOD's Providence more touching than that which shows Him watching and caring for us in the hour of temptation.

Finally St. Paul assures us that with every temptation there is the way of escape that we may be able to bear it—observe *the* way (for in the Greek the article is prefixed). There is always some one thing which, if we do, we shall be able to stand against the force of our temptation. It differs in various individuals in different temptations. Sometimes it is a duty which we are shrinking from, and which we are trying to persuade ourselves is not necessary in our case. Sometimes it is some Sacrament or means of grace which we are neglecting, but whatever it may be, remember there is always *the* way of escape, not that we may flee from the difficulty but that we may be able to bear it. How different from what many suppose; they pray that their trial may be taken away. GOD does not promise this in all cases, only that a way shall be made that they may be able to bear it—not to get rid of it as they wished, at least not till it has done its work in them.

"*Blessed are they which are persecuted for righteousness' sake: for their's is the kingdom of heaven.*"

I have already reminded you that this beatitude, which is not properly one of the series, foretells to us the result both *here* and *hereafter* of living by those seven laws of sanctity which precede it. The result *here* we have dwelt on at some length, it is persecution, suffering, temptation. but *hereafter* it is the Kingdom of heaven, that kingdom of glory in which not only Christ shall reign supreme, but those who are His shall reign with Him. There is a relationship between these two results; for the Cross is the key which is to unlock that kingdom. Without that Cross here how can we enter that kingdom hereafter?

The prophecy of Isaiah says of our Lord, "*The* KEY *of the house of David will I lay upon His shoulder.*" That Key was our Lord's Cross which He bore for us and with which He opened the kingdom of heaven to all believers, that Key we must all of us bear. How different were the Saints in character, in intellect, in rank and station here, but there was one common feature, they all bore upon their shoulder the Key of the Kingdom, the Cross which Christ gave them, and now "theirs is the Kingdom of heaven." What words can ever tell of the glories of that Kingdom, where the merciful shall have obtained mercy, where the pure in heart shall fear no further possibility of the stain of sin, where a peace shall reign which no discordant note can ever break, where those who have hungered and thirsted for Christ shall indeed be filled. Think of that great day when persecution shall be over for ever, and the dawn of that Kingdom shall drive away the darkness of this world! The Judge's great white throne is set up, surrounding it a rainbow of countless, dazzling shades, and all around, circle after circle of those who, having been through much tribulation, have washed their robes and made them white in the Blood of the Lamb. Saints, Martyrs, Virgins, Confessors, Patriarchs, Prophets, those who passed lives of toil and sorrow here on earth, all who were persecuted for righteousness' sake,—not only these, but all the Holy Angels,—they too stand around.

The earth reels and passes away, the rocks fall, the stars pale, the elements melt with fervent heat. Hark to the songs of the Angels! Look at that splendid court assembling in the skies! See the King Jesus coming in His Glory! See the shades of the night of the world flee away before the brightness of His presence!

How sweet those words of welcome spoken by the King of Saints, "*Come ye blessed of My Father inherit the Kingdom prepared for you from the foundation of the world.*" But how can human words tell of that kingdom of which the Holy Spirit says, "*Eye hath not seen, nor ear heard, neither have entered into the heart of man, the things which God hath prepared for them that love Him.*" Such is the kingdom which we are to enter by mounting the ladder of the beatitudes. Is it not worth while to tread the pathway of Sanctity, though it may need toil, and may bring persecution on us? Step by step we may mount up, each step not only bringing us nearer to the prize, but having its special blessing even in this life. Poverty, Mourning, Meekness, Desire for Christ, Mercy, Purity, Peace, Persecution, and then, then the Kingdom !!

BY THE SAME AUTHOR.

HELPS TO MEDITATION.

SKETCHES FOR EVERY DAY IN THE YEAR. With Introduction by the Right Rev. the Bishop of Springfield.

VOL. I., Advent to Trinity, 220 Meditations...... $2.50

VOL. II., Trinity to Advent, 200 Meditations, with copious indexes of the whole work.... $2.50

LAWS OF PENITENCE.

Addresses on the Seven Sayings of our Blessed Lord on the Cross............................45 cts.

FORTY HYMN TUNES.

(WITH WORDS.)

Paper...50 cts.
Cloth, gilt lettering..............................75 cts.

BENEDICITE OMNIA OPERA.

Set to Eighth Tone with various Endings and Faux Bourdons...........................15 cts.

www.ingramcontent.com/pod-product-compliance
Lightning Source LLC
Chambersburg PA
CBHW022137160426
43197CB00009B/1319